PENGUIN BOOKS

FITZGERALD DID IT

Meg Wolitzer is the author of several novels including *Surrender, Dorothy*, for which she is writing the screenplay for Showtime, *This Is Your Life*, which was the basis for Nora Ephron's film *This Is My Life*, as well as *Friends for Life*, *Sleeepwalking*, and *Hidden Pictures*. She received a grant from the National Endowment for the Arts in 1994, and in 1998 she had a story chosen for *Best American Short Stories* and *The Pushcart Prize*. She has taught writing workshops at the University of Iowa Writers' Workshop, Boston University, Skidmore College, the University of Houston, and Bennington College. She is currently writing an original screenplay. Meg Wolitzer lives in New York City.

D0517996

Fitzgerald
Did It

THE WRITER'S GUIDE TO
MASTERING THE SCREENPLAY

Meg Wolitzer

PENGUIN BOOKS

PENGUIN BOOKS
Published by the Penguin Group
Penguin Putnam Inc., 375 Hudson Street,
New York, New York 10014, U.S.A.
Penguin Books Ltd, 27 Wrights Lane, London W8 5TZ, England
Penguin Books Australia Ltd, Ringwood, Victoria, Australia
Penguin Books Canada Ltd, 10 Alcorn Avenue,
Toronto, Ontario, Canada M4V 3B2
Penguin Books (N.Z.) Ltd, 182–190 Wairau Road,
Auckland 10, New Zealand

Penguin Books Ltd, Registered Offices:
Harmondsworth, Middlesex, England

First published in Penguin Books 1999

3 5 7 9 10 8 6 4 2

LIBRARY OF CONGRESS CATALOGING IN PUBLICATION DATA
Wolitzer, Meg.
Fitzgerald did it : the writer's guide to mastering the screenplay /
by Meg Wolitzer.
p.   cm.
Filmography: p.
Includes bibliographical references.
ISBN 0 14 02.7576 2
1. Motion picture plays—Technique.   2. Motion picture
authorship.   I. Title.
PN1996.W63   1999
808.2'3—dc21   98-47044

Printed in the United States of America
Set in New Caledonia
Designed by Betty Lew

CONTENTS

CONTENTS

Fitzgerald
Did It

In Fitzgerald's Footsteps

Every writer I know loves going to the movies. There's intense pleasure to be had in dropping everything and heading to the triplex to watch a movie of any kind—whether it's refined and subtle and takes place in an English manor house, or overblown and shameless and takes place in another galaxy. While many of us are probably more discriminating in our choice of reading material, we tend to be cheerfully broad-minded when it comes to the movies we see. Sometimes, an unlikely movie can have a surprising and lasting effect.

As a child I was terrified by but obsessed with the 1958 Vincent Price movie *The Fly*, in which a scientist accidentally becomes half man, half bug. Whenever the movie came on TV (usually after school on the 4:30 movie) I would sit in front of our black-and-white set with my fingers forming a weave in front of my eyes, blocking out the most frightening parts but unwilling to miss the whole thing. The famous ending, in which the fly is discovered in the yard with the head of the scientist on it, now old and white-haired and crying in a tinny, high-pitched voice, *"Hellllp me! Hellllp me!"* became an image I often thought about when I began writing fiction years later. I'm not exactly sure why that movie obsessed me so, but for whatever reason it became part of my interior life, insinuating itself into my writer's imagination. Since then, dozens of movies have occupied that role in various ways—because they were frightening, moving, funny, unbearably sad or extremely vivid. All the writers I know have spoken of movies they have seen—everything from *The Mummy's Hand* to *The Piano*—that had a profound effect on them and their work.

Like most people, writers are drawn to movies because they entertain, because they educate, because they provide a release and, finally, because they are visual—all traits that might be used to describe writing, too, such as the short story, novel, play, magazine article or personal essay. But perhaps the most notable reason that writers are drawn to movies—and one that causes them to want to take a stab at writing their own screenplays—is that every movie tells a story, and writers always respond to a good story. Whether telling one ourselves, or sitting back and letting someone else do the telling, we understand that stories are essential to a vivid interior life.

It's been my experience that every writer, at one time or another, considers writing a screenplay. There's a great tradition behind such urges, although I hope that your own interest doesn't spring from desperation, the way F. Scott Fitzgerald's largely did. In 1937, when Fitzgerald went to Hollywood, he did so under the burden of overwhelming financial strains that included expenses for his wife Zelda's mental illness. He died three years later, but in the interim he contributed in a minor capacity to many films, including *Gone With the Wind*, supposedly writing the scene in which Rhett receives the bonnet he then gives to Scarlett. Fitzgerald isn't remembered for his "bonnet" scene, of course, or for anything else he wrote for Hollywood, but I'm certain that he, like most novelists, saw his screen work as entirely separate from his fiction, and strove to keep the two from overlapping. This is a good attitude for a writer to take; sometimes, when a real overlap occurs, a writer becomes confused, and everything he or she produces feels dissatisfying.

But when it's all kept separate—when a novel's a novel and a screenplay's a screenplay—then the work can be pleasurable. If a fiction writer, journalist or playwright really wants to try writing a screenplay, he or she definitely should, preferably when the catalyst for doing so isn't desperation or a spouse's mounting psychiatric bills.

Of course, it's always been difficult for writers to make a living in a so-called pure fashion. Some writers find themselves subsidizing their writing by choosing an academic life that involves a tenured position at a sleepy college (weekly faculty meetings aren't the worst thing in the world), or else going a completely different route: Hollywood.

Several years ago, when I decided to write my first screenplay, I was (and I still am) primarily a novelist who had had the good fortune of having one of my books made into a movie. *This Is My Life* (based on my novel *This Is Your Life*) was directed by Nora Ephron and co-written by Ephron and her sister Delia. While I wasn't involved in the actual writing of the movie, Nora Ephron graciously gave me a window into the ongoing creative process. It was tremendously exciting to spend some time on the movie set (Toronto standing in for New York City) and watch my characters Dottie, Opal and Erica come to life. After the movie wrapped, I decided that I would give screenwriting a try.

The following year, I began work on the simultaneous novel and screenplay versions of *Friends for Life*, with Nora Ephron attached as director. At first, I had no idea of where I was going, and absolutely no innate understanding of the rhythms of a movie. My screenplay scenes were talk, talk, talk, and while the writing in them was intermittently lively and fresh, something was wrong. I wasn't sure what it was.

I decided, at that point, that I needed to tutor myself in the basics of how to write a script. Like most people who undertake a screenplay, I went to the bookstore to purchase a few screenwriting guides. The assortment that I found on the shelf was staggering; there was a tremendous glut of books to choose from, and while at first I was astonished by the Heinz 57–like variety, as I stood leafing through them I began to notice a trend: all of these books were geared toward people who had not only no screenwriting experience but also very little writing experience of *any* kind.

While some of the books were useful in different ways, much of the information imparted in them included the sort of advice that I had learned long ago in my first creative writing class in college. The books dwelled at length on the rudiments of character development and dialogue, assuming that the reader has had no prior knowledge of these elements. For an experienced writer, this was tedious reading. There was an awful lot to slog through before getting to anything new. Also, there were no protections offered to the seasoned writer—protections against his or her own tendency to write in a writerly rather than visually directed fashion. I wanted very much to learn how to write a screenplay, but I knew that the books that were out there weren't quite right for me.

Through a combination of patience, trial and error, and many hours clocked reading other screenplays, I have been cobbling together a career that involves scriptwriting as well as writing novels. I learned that some of the problems I'd had with *Friends for Life* had to do with my tendency to see a screenplay as a collection of scenes, rather than a carefully assembled piece of writing with one definite direction. Slowly, I got better at it. I will probably never be as natural a screenwriter as I am a novelist but I've been making a steady living from it, and I've learned both how to use my writing strengths when I craft a screenplay, and how to abandon the tics and old habits that could weaken my scripts.

As you already know, the best way to become a better writer is to pay attention to other people's writing. When writers go to the movies, we intuitively respond to the *writing* onscreen; we are almost never unaware of the fact that, for every five minutes of screen time, some writer had to create five pages of writing. In the cool darkness of a theater, while all around us other people are deeply absorbed in the pleasures of the movie, happily unaware of the extensive craft that went into it, we often find ourselves preoccupied with the question: How did they do it? And, more to the point: How can I do it?

Contemporary writers such as Richard Price, Pete Dexter, Wendy Wasserstein, Scott Spencer and Roy Blount have all written for Hollywood, as have fleets of other writers. (Just check the membership list of the Writers' Guild of America, the union that all screenwriters belong to, and you'll see many familiar names from the bookstore shelves.) As with Fitzgerald, the desire to write screenplays sometimes springs from our basest impulse: to make money. As we sit in our modest homes late into the night, working on the third draft of a short story for which some minuscule literary magazine will pay us a hundred dollars and three free copies of the issue, we begin to dream of a lusher existence that involves manservants, tropical drinks at the Polo Lounge and immediate occupancy of the house that used to belong to Rita Hayworth.

But usually there's something else going on, too: a sense of *I can do this*. A sense that, because we already know how to write well, it stands to reason that we ought to be able to write a solid and saleable screenplay. *The Postman* sucked! we think to ourselves. And even *The Wings of the Dove* wasn't all it was cracked up to be. So many movies are disappointing, we think, and *they* somehow managed to get made. After all, we figure, not only do we know how to write well, but we are infinitely better writers than many of those people living in L.A. who do nothing for a living but crank out screenplay after soulless screenplay.

I want to say up front that this is a misconception. Like most people attempting a screenplay, writers often fail miserably at first. But what's particularly significant is that writers often fail *similarly*. They bump up against the same kinds of problems again and again, obstacles not always faced by the novice writer. To generalize, writers' initial screenplays tend to be talky, static, interior and structurally shaky. (Certainly my own were.) The ability to write well does not automatically guarantee that you can write a screenplay, a form that is more often about architecture and imagery and movement than it is about language.

When Richard Price was recently asked what influence his screenplays have had on his fiction, he answered, "None." Every screenwriting impulse applied to a novel is a disaster, he said. And every novel impulse applied to a screenplay is a disaster. Fiction is concerned with language. Screenplays are about giving a story momentum. I think this reply gets right to the heart of the matter. Those writers who morph into the most natural screenwriters are the ones who are already married to the idea of story, and who are able to treat their actual words dispassionately, including and discarding them as necessary.

As a writer with some experience in other forms, you are definitely starting out with special skills that will help you as you go along. But you are also starting out with some handicaps: your own perception of your strengths, and the assumption that you will know how to apply them in your new role as screenwriter. The truth is more complex than this. The talents that you've already honed *can* be put into service as you hammer out a script, but in most other ways you are a beginner, and some of your long-held assumptions about writing are, in various ways, actually a handicap.

This book, geared specifically toward people who already know how to write, will provide an intuitive rather than scientific method for writing screenplays. It's intended for novelists, short-story writers, essayists and journalists, among others—anyone who has a grasp of some of the complex and subtle points of writing, yet who isn't sure how to translate his or her abilities into the language of the screen. (I want to add a caveat here: I'm going to be taking a fairly conventional route in these pages, deconstructing the conventional screenplay as opposed to anything truly idiosyncratic or groundbreaking. If you're planning on creating something startlingly unusual that defies the rules, you'll have to figure it out on your own.)

Fitzgerald Did It will skip the things you already know about writing, and focus on the specific ways your knowledge can be redirected as you write a script. I hope it will help you overcome the stumbling blocks of talkiness and structural weakness that many experienced writers come upon when they turn their attention to the movies.

Although screenwriting won't ever feel nearly as fluent a process to me as writing novels, I take real pride in working on scripts. I've learned (and I admit this somewhat sheepishly) that writing a screenplay can be as gratifying as writing a novel. There's a structural beauty to a well-organized script, and if you're able to master the structure and fill it with absorbing, original content, you will have created something that might actually become a film. Although in my opinion the screenplay is usually more a matter of craft than of art, there's still an enormous sense of accomplishment to be had when you've done it right (especially if you've been able to keep it separate from your other work, never confusing the two). Some people feel that their screenplays actually enhance their other work, giving it a stronger sense of story.

So maybe Fitzgerald's particular experiences in Hollywood aren't exactly something to aspire to. But regardless of his personal misery, Fitzgerald was a writer who was willing to make the shift from one form to another. Fortunately, you don't need to move to Hollywood anymore to write screenplays; you can do it all from the squalor and comfort of your own home, and in these pages I will try to show you how.

Chapter One

Big Ideas and How to Structure Them

Perhaps one of the reasons you became a writer is the freedom attached—not only the freedom inherent in a job that allows you to nap when you need to and wear whatever *shmatah* you want all day, but also the freedom to invent the rules as you go along. If you're a fiction writer, you know that your short story may be ten pages long, or it may be eighty. Of course, if it starts to head into that upper range, you may suddenly decide to tell everyone it's a novella, but the point is that you can go on for as long as you need to. Some novels today (the thick telephone books of David Foster Wallace, Thomas Pynchon, Don DeLillo) far exceed the traditional page limit or even the weight limit. Even magazine and newspaper articles have a way of stretching out if necessary, as do plays (*Angels in America*, for instance). In essence, many writers are given as long as they need to make their points, and are permitted to make these points in the free-associative way that they think best.

This is not true of screenwriters. Freedom of length and form are not among the pleasures of writing a screenplay. Many writers initially find it extremely difficult to adhere to the fairly inflexible structure of the three-act script—referred to in other screenwriting manuals as "the paradigm." But the more you work within the structure, coming to understand it and to see why it's so essential to the success of your script, the more naturally it will come to you.

STRUCTURE

A screenplay is a fairly simple piece of architecture—definitely Mission rather than Rococo. Most mainstream scripts are around 120 pages long (often even shorter, and occasionally longer), and those 120 pages are broken up into three discrete acts. Somewhere between pages 20 and 30, there is the introduction of a *plot point*—an occurrence within the story that sends the script off in an entirely new direction, in effect ending the first act and leading into the second. Another plot point is introduced at the end of act two—around page 90—to end the second act and start the third. There may be additional plot points in your script, especially if the story is heavily plotted, but there will *always* be plot points in the places I've mentioned, which serve to shift the story into a new, necessary direction and create Richard Price's notion of "momentum."

No screenwriting book would be complete without some sort of diagram in it to make the whole process appear technically sophisticated. I plan to keep diagrams to a bare minimum in this volume—because I often think they're much ado about nothing, such as:

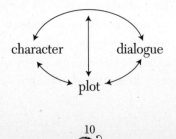

But the diagram I'm about to show you is both simple and essential. There will be times when you are lost in the middle of a screenplay, and if you can stop at these moments, stand back and visualize the three-act structure—the beauty and economy of its design and how well it serves the story—you will soon be able to find your way.

The Three-Act Structure

Act One	Act Two	Act Three
(pp. 1–30)	(pp. 30–90)	(pp. 90–120)
The setup.	The conflict.	The resolution.

Plot point   *Plot point*
(leading up to p. 30)   (leading up to p. 90)

I'll go into this diagram in more detail later, but for now, you need to know that the first thirty pages of the script (give or take a few pages) serve to set up the characters and their situation and the story. Pages 30 through 90 establish the conflict, sometimes known as the confrontation, and pages 90 through 120 resolve all the unresolved material. This may seem abstract and confusing right now, especially if you haven't seen the need for such close attention to structure in the other forms of writing you've done. But the more you work on your screenplay, the more sense it will make.

I was initially very resistant to learning about structure, preferring to rely on some nebulous, innate sense of "organization" to guide me through. (I think I've always been this way, having been a good student early in life and impressing my teachers. It gave me the false sense that I could always do things my own way—sometimes taking shortcuts—and still succeed. By ninth grade, this was no longer true. And when it comes to screenwriting, it certainly isn't true.) For now, you should familiarize yourself objectively and impersonally with the overarching sense of screenplay structure, and we'll return to it again when we start mapping out your script in chapter three.

WHERE DO YOU GET YOUR IDEAS?

This, as you no doubt already know, is the question that writers are most frequently asked during the Q & A sessions after readings, or when cornered at cocktail parties, and it's perhaps one of the most maddening questions we can be asked, too, because there's no single good answer. Ideas, of course, are never transmitted to a writer via some sort of creativity satellite, but instead are developed through a subterranean mixture of experiences, interests, obsessions and other factors. Yet what inspires a short story or magazine article is often completely different from what inspires a screenplay. Ultimately, a script isn't meant to be read; it's meant, in its final form, to be watched, and in addition to all the other qualities it must have, it needs to possess an irresistible watchability. This is a term that you ought to keep in mind as you write; never lose sight of the fact that a script should seduce the reader through its visual drama.

In a work of fiction or some other medium meant only to be read, you can include entire passages whose sole reason to be there lies in language, character or place. Molly Bloom's soliloquy at the end of *Ulysses* goes on for pages, and William Faulkner (who worked for Howard Hawks as a screenwriter/drinking buddy in Hollywood in the 1940s) never met a paragraph he could bear to bring to an end.

Fiction writers are given tacit license to take a sharp or subtle detour that doesn't detract from the work as a whole, but instead obliquely gives it a freshness, a distinctive vision or voice. This is not true for screenwriters. If a scene exists only to show us something about the way a husband and wife talk to each other, or the way a character feels about her mother, or even to demonstrate how well the screenwriter can flex his or her language muscle—and if it does not further the point of the movie in an irresistibly watchable manner—it probably has no business being in your screenplay. Beautiful, telling and well written though it may be, it might well pull your movie down to the ocean floor. *Take it out.* Better yet, never put it in to begin with.

Through your script, you need to convey something that will be perceived by an audience as urgent business; they must feel that they cannot take their eyes off the screen. This is different from the experience you've already had as a writer; you understand that while you need to create an interest in the reader of articles, stories or books, reading is a stop-and-start activity. The assumption of a reader's leisureliness is built into the writer's task. There is time, in a novel or a long essay, to include sections that give the reader a break, perhaps immediately following a section that is particularly disturbing or intense. In most forms of writing, these lighter, more reflective sections provide a kind of sorbet to clear the palate between courses. There is some latitude, some allowance to run on for a while, to shift gears. *In a screenplay, every word counts.* (In that respect, perhaps the writer who will make the transition into movies most easily is the writer of haiku, forever locked into a seventeen-syllable limit.)

But what sort of material is "irresistibly watchable"? What

sort of ideas will present you with the sufficient tensions you will need both on the page and onscreen? And where do you go about finding them? As you begin to consider these questions, you may feel you've regressed slightly, back to the doggedly earnest beginning writer you once were. Essentially, *you* now need to be the one asking the somewhat naive question, *"Where do you get your ideas?"* You will find that it's an entirely different question—and a necessary one—when we're talking about screenplays.

HIGH CONCEPT AND LOW CONCEPT

These terms, which are tossed around in Hollywood as freely as a pizza at Spago, may be preoccupying you right now, as you root around to find a subject to which to devote an entire screenplay. I think such terms are perilous to writers, and I wish that they never existed. It would be so much better if all screenwriters could simply lose themselves in the pleasure of the subject that absorbs them the most. But no one writes in a vacuum. You shouldn't become overly distracted by these worries right now, but it's okay to take a small, orienting side-trip into thinking about the "size" of your concept.

Let's say you want to write a screenplay that someone might buy, but you don't want to be the type of screenwriter who will do virtually anything to make money, hammering out *Meatballs XII* or *Great-Grandfather of the Bride*, or *I Know What You Did Eight Summers Ago*. You want to write a movie you actually care about, the kind of movie that you would like to go see. But somewhere in your cerebral cortex lies the inevitable knowledge that if you submit your script to a studio, it will be judged not only on its quality, but on whether it's a high-concept script, or a decidely low-concept one. At times it seems as though the universe of movies roughly breaks into two camps: (a) those about a troubled but kindhearted farmer struggling to keep his land and (b) those about a group of terrorists who take over the Mall of America.

You know that scripts in camp b, the high-concept camp, have a better chance of being produced, while those in camp a, the low-concept camp, need to win someone over with their charm, emotional resonance or the fact that Leonardo DiCaprio has expressed an interest in playing the part of the troubled but kindhearted farmer.

As you think about the movie you really want to write, make a list of the movies you have enjoyed the most in your life. Where would you place them—under the "high" or "low" category? If most of your favorite movies are definitely high concept—containing an easily explained idea that presents a problem and then solves it through a sequence of exciting scenes—then probably your first foray into movies ought to be a high-concept idea, something that naturally draws you in, and which you likely have an intuitive ability to write. (I'm a big advocate of a writer's employing his or her intuition throughout the writing process—it's something that can't be taught in a creative writing workshop or at the UCLA film school.) If, on the other hand, your favorite movies tend to be the small, quiet ones starring Sam Waterston or Amanda Plummer, perhaps you ought to lean in that direction. Although it probably is more difficult to sell a low-concept movie, that shouldn't stop you from writing a good movie that engages you. There are all sorts of ways to sell a script, and some lower-concept scripts get picked up by bankable stars, who in effect can push a reluctant studio to make the movie. Whether your script gets bought or made is another story entirely, and pretty much out of your control. The factors that *are* in your control are the following: how well written and well structured your script is; whether it has a beginning, a middle and an end; and whether it is irresistibly watchable.

It's a mistake for a writer to set out to write a "high-concept" movie merely because it seems to stand a better chance of getting made or doing big box office. It almost never works when you approach it this way. I'm reminded of a few serious writers I know who have consciously set out to write best-sellers, often under pseudonyms. They've become veritable students of commercial fiction, reading everything by Danielle Steel or Tom Clancy, but when they actually write such a book themselves, it almost never works. The book is rejected by publishers, who say that the manuscript is lacking something basic, although they can't put their finger on what it is.

I think what these books are lacking is conviction. The difference between a writer of literary fiction attempting one of these books and Danielle Steel doing so is that Danielle Steel actually believes in her stories and her characters. She is fully absorbed in them when she's writing, and she doesn't look down on them or think of them as merely a conduit to money and success.

This isn't to say that you can't write a high-concept movie. You certainly can, if your intuition leads you there, and more power to you if it does, but the idea needs to arise the same way a low-concept idea would: out of genuine conviction and interest, and an innate sense that your idea would make a terrific film.

HUNTING AND GATHERING

What sort of material generates enthusiasm and excitement? And where do you go about finding it? The following is a partial list of the metaphorical fields and streams in which to locate a subject for a screenplay:

- **Personal Experience**. Were you ever in a place that struck you, at the time you were there or perhaps in retrospect, as very visually compelling? This might mean Pamplona or a cowboy bar in Texas. But it certainly means a place that resonated at the time, and that has stayed with you ever since, either positively or negatively. Writers possess a useful tool called intuition; if you have the hunch that a place would be visually compelling onscreen, you're probably right. You might also look through old photo albums to see what places have inspired you to take the most photographs.

    Similarly, a job you've held or an activity you've participated in may make for a good jumping-off point in a screenplay. The problem is that people are often so close to their experiences that they may have a difficult time separating themselves from those experiences in order to see them as they might appear in a screenplay.

    I once spent some time with a friend who wanted to generate an idea for a movie. We talked extensively about various byzantine plots she had come up with, some of them involving stolen jewels and elaborate drug-running schemes. I tried to help her make one of these plots work to her advantage, but I didn't hold out much hope for this, because she didn't really know much about the subjects she was mentioning, nor did she seem particularly impassioned about them.

Finally, at the end of one of our discussions, she mentioned—almost in passing—that she was off to see her "ex-politician father." I asked her what she meant, and she told me something I hadn't known—that her father had been involved with the Nixon presidency and, tangentially, with Watergate. She began to regale me with stories of what it had been like to grow up in her household during that period of history. In five minutes, she created a world much more complex and compelling than that previous, artificial-sounding universe of drug smugglers and jewel thieves. It was clear to me that she was capable of writing a good screenplay about a child watching her father become entangled in scandal and shame. She could certainly change enough of the details so as not to embarrass her father; unlike most people, she had been given a privileged glimpse at a subject that was rich with visual and dramatic possibilities. But what was astonishing to me was that it hadn't occurred to her that this might be something worth writing about.

As you think about starting your screenplay, you should remember that a fact that you may take for granted about yourself—something you grew up with or lived through or have learned about, something that is so familiar to you now as to be commonplace—might be just the thing that would be compelling in a screenplay.

- **Creating a "Curriculum Vitae."** This is a good time to put together a special kind of résumé (for your eyes only), in which you look through your life chronologically, writing down the pivotal events and facts and realizations that have shaped you. These might range from such a seemingly small event (although not small to you) as having gotten your first period while traveling with your family in Greece, to as large an event as the death of someone you loved. Your CV will provide a guide that you can refer to whenever you need to be reminded of your own experience, and the ways in which some of it might be used to your advantage.

Of course, not everyone wants to write about themselves. It is perfectly reasonable for a writer to say—as one recently said to me—"I'm a very private person. When I write, I want it to be about something completely different." I respect and understand this point of view, but I feel that I have to add a caveat here: If you haven't put yourself into your work, then your work won't feel authentic. But what I mean by "yourself" isn't necessarily your literal self or your literal experience. The self can be disguised and altered and entirely transformed, and in the best work it often is.

Suppose, for example, that my friend with the ex-politician father really isn't interested in writing about Watergate or that difficult time in her family's life. Suppose she has already spent much of her life thinking about the topic and discussing it endlessly and weepily in therapy, and now she is sick to death of both Watergate and that creepy, paranoid Nixon. As far as she's concerned, the idea of undertaking a project about that long-ago historical moment is completely unappealing. Suppose she tells me that she really *does* want to write about a drug smuggler. Isn't there any way, she wants to know, that she can make this topic seem believable?

If this were the case, then I would ask her to examine her fascination with crime in order to discover its origin. All writers need to be historians of a sort, looking at the places from which ideas arrive, and tracing their paths. Let's say that my friend has already told me that no one she knows is a drug smuggler, and that she merely likes watching those kinds of crime/intrigue movies because she finds them exciting. I would still feel compelled to ask her: Where are *you* in all of this? And I would assume that she is, in fact, somewhere within this idea for a movie, even in a much-removed capacity. Because I now have certain information about her background, I would start to think about her father the politician. Back during the Nixon administration, when he became caught up in the government scandal, did he, in fact, *feel* like a criminal? And did his family see him that way, too? Was criminality something that began to interest her around this time? If she can locate the heart of her interest in her subject, then she'll be able to give it real direction, which is essential to all good writing.

- **The Most Unforgettable Character I Ever Met**. *Tender Mercies*, *Terms of Endearment*, *Shine*, *Sling Blade*: these are all movies with a unique character at their core. While going into a movie studio and proudly announcing that you have written a character-driven screenplay is probably the kiss of death (it will be immediately translated to mean "noncommercial," those specific titles mentioned notwithstanding), character is a respectable place to start thinking about a movie you want to write.

I'd like to make the distinction here between the kind of character you might choose as a protagonist in a piece of fiction and the kind that works well in a movie. While initially, the form a screenplay takes is a written one, the goal is for it eventually to be brought to life and dramatized by a group of actors. A character in a character-driven movie really *does* need to be larger-than-life; his or her literary counterpart, however, may be smaller and less boldly defined, and still be able to hold our interest.

If you're a writer who's used to being extremely subtle in a short story or essay, it may come as a shock to have to abandon that method now. But certain flagrant character traits, whether they're homophobia (*As Good as It Gets*), narcissism (*Terms of Endearment*) or wanton recklessness (*Primary Colors*), can fill up the screen in a satisfying way. There's something that happens onscreen—a kind of sucking up of energy—that creates a need for an excess of that energy to be put in in the first place. It's the character equivalent of movie makeup; while an actress wearing full makeup might look like a hooker if she walked down the street, she needs to wear this makeup onscreen merely to look alive. Characters in a movie need to be themselves—only more so.

- **Mrs. O'Leary's Cow**. This refers to the cow that supposedly kicked over a lantern and started the Chicago fire of 1871; often, in a movie, you will notice that there is a single, defining event that triggers a host of unexpected consequences. (Think of *Rear Window*, in which James Stewart has broken his leg and is forced to spend a lot of time in a wheelchair. Bored and miserable, he starts to notice strange goings-on in the apartment building across the way.) A good method to get started shaping an idea is to come up with an equivalent event.
- **Obsessions and Compulsions**. What obsesses you— what really absorbs your interest—might make for a per-

fect movie, if you are willing to mold it appropriately. (*Vertigo*, *Field of Dreams* and *Fatal Attraction* all rely on—but manage to transcend—characters' obsessions.) Very few ideas from life are fit for the screen as is; most need molding of some sort in order to make them more cinematic, more dramatic, more structurally sound and, most of the time, more interesting. What obsesses you may not obsess me.

Someone (I forget who) once said that the topic of homosexuality is a lot like beekeeping: fascinating to those who practice it, mundane to those who don't. As a screenwriter, your job is to take *your* version of homosexuality or beekeeping, and make it riveting; what obsesses you may really interest me if you show me *why* it's so fascinating to you. Never take it for granted that I would be interested too. The charm of a movie such as 1979's *Breaking Away* lay in the fact that we were given a crash course in its central subject (bicycle racing), and by the end of the movie we really cared whether or not the appealing young hero won the big race. We experienced the vicarious pleasure of bicycle racing, not necessarily because we had experienced it ourselves but because the screenwriter, the late Steve Tesich, led us into the protagonist's obsessions, and as a result a whole world opened up.

- **A Story That "Tells Itself."** There are some story lines that seem to roll themselves out like a long, glorious carpet (*The Shawshank Redemption*, *Pulp Fiction*, *Broadway Danny Rose*). Identifying such a story line takes skill. But often, what's there will still need some further unrolling and retooling in order to make it work as a screenplay.

For instance, you might have grown up hearing nostalgic stories of your mother's Brooklyn girlhood. You might have heard about the way the whole neighborhood rallied during World War II when the boy next door was killed in active duty, and how his outgoing, card-playing parents became totally different people, withdrawing into themselves and quitting the Saturday-night neighborhood canasta game. Maybe your mother, almost unaware of what she was doing, helped them come out of their depression.

This description has elements of a movie about it: keen visuals, articulated characters and the ready-made drama inherent in war. You might think that such a story will just "write itself." But remember, nothing ever writes itself. The story that seems to be writing itself is probably not doing as good a job as the writer could do.

STARTING TO WRITE

Maybe you've been thinking and thinking and you decide that you really do like your girlhood-in-wartime-Brooklyn movie, which from here on in shall be dubbed *Bay Parkway*. It's visual, it's visceral, it's both sad and funny, it has great parts for male and female leads and, best of all, it's the kind of movie that you would definitely go see. So can you start your screenplay yet?

Probably not. Because even though there's something intriguing about the premise and the characters, the *beats* of the story aren't there yet—the important moments that propel the movie along. Also, none of the scenes have been established, nor the so-called arc of the main character (i.e., the changes the character undergoes over the course of the film).

The subplot (or subplots) isn't there either—the inextricably related secondary story that will weave through the script in order to heighten the tensions of the primary story. (More on that later.) It's possible that, if you sat down right now to write *Bay Parkway*, scene after scene would fall into place and your characters would simply spring to life like sponges dropped into water, but chances are that after a few pages your movie would become disorganized and rudderless.

If you're like most writers I know, you would probably insist that you're capable of starting right now, and that everything will simply come to you as you write. You might say that you're used to plunging in and muddling your way through, and that you just want to be left alone to figure it out as you go along. In fact, I *have* often told my fiction students to dive right in when they have an urge to begin a story or novel. I've reassured them that one of three things will likely happen: they will find their own voice as they go along, or the characters will lead them to what the story is about, or else the language will. I've instructed them not to worry at this point about that nuisance known as structure; it's something they can think about much later, long after they've piled on the interesting language and the unusual characters.

None of this applies to screenwriters. In the world of screenplays, *structure is everything*. I can tell you from experience that if you attempt to figure out your entire script during the actual writing of a draft, you will cost yourself much more time in the long run, because you will have to keep going back over and over the same material until it becomes coherent and streamlined.

Writers long for a moment of instant gratification, and such moments are few and far between. I tend to be extremely eager to get started on a new project; when I come up with an idea, I want to drop everything and begin work, even if I'm in the middle of making dinner or playing Monopoly with my children. But this is a bad impulse—more "Goofus" than "Gallant," if you remember the old *Highlights for Children* magazine cartoon. (Goofus interrupts his own wedding ceremony to begin writing his actual screenplay; Gallant waits until after the honeymoon is over just to begin working on an outline.) When an idea arrives, you may have the feeling that it just can't wait. In fact, it *can* wait, and the more you think about it and find a way to organize it, the better shape it will be in.

INDEX CARDS

Many people choose to use index cards to show the scenes in a script; on each card, they write a significant moment in the movie, such as: "Alice gets on the subway train and sees the newspaper headline." The cards can be shuffled and reshuffled according to need, or tacked to the wall so that the movie can literally be "seen" before it's written. Many screenwriters swear by this method, saying that it allows them an infinite number of possibilities. They lie on a couch in the den and experiment with a variety of combinations. For them, the cards allow for a certain kind of flexibility of imagination. Seeing all the scenes in front of them reminds them that movies are comprised of scenes—that scenes provide the foundation, and if those scenes are reordered, the movie will have a different feel to it.

Personally, coming from a prose background, I tend to think in a more linear fashion, and I'm resistant to the use of cards. (Not to mention the fact that I live in a typical New

York City apartment with no den.) If index cards work for you, great. But some writers I know who make forays into film choose to take another path toward writing the script, a way more in keeping with their strengths: writing a detailed treatment.

THE TREATMENT

A treatment is essentially a breakdown of your movie that runs anywhere from a page or two to twenty pages (or even more, depending on the density of the script). Often, if a producer or a studio executive is interested in an idea, he or she may ask for a treatment first, rather than have to pay for the writer to complete an actual script.

A treatment, while often an extremely tedious exercise for a writer who is champing at the bit, is a very valuable document both for you and for someone who's interested in hiring you. *A treatment is a blueprint for a screenplay.* It provides you with a kind of connect-the-dots format that will make it easier in the long run for you to write your script. You may be very antsy to get started on the screenplay, and perhaps you fear that writing a treatment will bog you down in details and take too long. This is what I thought when I was starting out, and I had vivid memories of the pointless outlines I used to write in my teacher Miss Mango's fourth-grade class, detailing the social studies unit my class was studying at the time ("Ancient Greece: A. The people. 1. Wearing togas. 2. Building temples . . ."). Though the tedium may be unavoidable, my fears of the pointlessness of writing a treatment turned out to be unfounded.

While some screenplays are character driven and others

are driven by tricky, complex language, a screenplay isn't held together by either its characters or its language. *Screenplays are held together by the connective tissue of the story.* A treatment spells out the story in the simplest, most vivid terms. It lets you see whether or not you actually *have* an adequate story in the first place, or whether the proposed script will be lacking in ways that you couldn't have anticipated. Over the course of the treatment, your characters and their arcs and perhaps even bits of the language of the script will be introduced; while these are inextricable from the quality of the story, they should never be thought of as substitutes.

There's a real difference between a treatment you write for your own use and one you write to interest a studio executive, producer or agent. If you're writing the treatment only for yourself—to use as a map to help you develop your script—then don't worry about length, or whether it seems too elaborate. More is actually *more* now, not less; if you work the details out during the treatment, then you'll have less confusion later on, when you're actually writing the script. But if you're writing your treatment expressly to show to someone else who might want to buy it or to represent you as an agent, then be sure that it's concise and cracklingly readable, and try to keep it to ten pages or less. The attention span of most readers in Hollywood is somewhere between that of a seven-year-old with ADD and a head of lettuce. This isn't an insult, entirely; when someone in the industry reads a treatment or a script, he or she is looking for one thing and one thing only: an original story, told well. Sometimes writers try to conceal the fact that they don't have a good story under a mountain of distracting prose.

Before you try writing a treatment, you ought to read one first. I've included a mock-treatment for a piece of movie fluff called *We Have to Stop*. In the chapter following the treatment, I'll deconstruct it and make suggestions for your own treatment.

For someone who's already a proficient writer, a treatment is a great resource to have. You know how to use language well; you know how to write good prose. Your treatment will most likely be a strong one, because you are already experienced in turning out blocks of descriptive writing. Your abilities will definitely assist you at this part of the process, so use them to their fullest. There are plenty of poorly written treatments floating around on the West Coast of this country, most executed by people who have little prose experience and no innate feel for writing. A well-crafted treatment will get you attention, and it can help you find your way through the story.

Chapter Two

A Sample Treatment

WE HAVE TO STOP

Set in Providence, Rhode Island, in and around Brown University and a local working-class neighborhood, *We Have to Stop* is a contemporary romantic comedy with a fantasy element, about two people overcoming the obstacles to love.

Act One

CARRIE JAMISON is an appealing, almost beautiful woman in her late twenties/early thirties—slightly unfocused and frazzled, but in a way that you forgive immediately. Carrie works as an assistant chef at a resturant and can't get over her ex-boyfriend, DAVID. She and David broke up a year ago but as time has passed and dates with other men have gone badly, David begins to look better than he actually was. Her best friend, CLAUDIA, sardonic, loyal and overweight, thinks David is really boring: "He sells *coasters*," she reminds Carrie.

TIM BOWLES is a flirtatious assistant professor of Comp. Lit. at Brown in his early thirties, teaching undergraduates and desperately trying to resist the temptation to sleep with students. He's limber and ironic, a jogger who always has to be doing something physical. Tim falls for inappropriate women: too young or married. The women he likes will never lead to a full life, which is what he wants, at least in the abstract. His best friend, biology professor LOU MARINO, is happily married and has a life of domestic disorder and love that Tim wishes he had, but it doesn't seem as though he ever will.

Both Carrie and Tim are unlucky when it comes to love. They're not malingering neurotics, but they have specific love-related problems that have sent them into therapy with a revered relationship expert, therapist DR. MILES JOSLIN. Dr. Joslin is a handsome, sleek, witty and cryptic but extremely compassionate middle-aged shrink with a pipe that he keeps stuffed with a rare Balkan tobacco that smells, according to Carrie, like a combination of "burning leaves and Froot Loops." Dr. Joslin feels that if you're going to be in his care, you need to follow his orders. His patients do; he's authoritarian but not a quack. Tim and Carrie have never met, but they've seen each other in passing (and have been attracted to each other) because he has the appointment after hers.

One day, as Carrie is in the middle of her session, Dr. Joslin starts to give her a very important piece of advice. "After months of listening to you, I think I know a way for you to be happy," he says. "Now listen very closely. Let me tell you something about love." She leans in. He leans in. And he keeps leaning. He falls off his leather chair and onto the Persian rug, clutching his chest.

Carrie screams his name, then rushes out into the waiting room, where Tim is sitting. She enlists his aid and together

they try to resuscitate their therapist, to no avail. The para-
medics arrive and declare Dr. Joslin dead of a heart attack.
Both patients are devastated.

In their shock, Carrie and Tim go to a nearby dive and
drink and talk about Dr. Joslin, trading weepy anecdotes.
Both of them were just approaching a turning point in therapy at which they were going to start being cured of their in-
timacy probems, but now Dr. Joslin is dead, and they feel
they will be stuck in relationship purgatory forever.

At the end of the night, because she can barely walk and
Tim lives around the corner, she goes home with him. Having had too much to drink, she passes out and they sleep side
by side in the bed. When morning comes, Carrie is disori-
ented, finding herself in a strange man's bed. To make matters worse, suddenly a woman lets herself into the house: it's
a sultry, aggressive student named LISA. She and Carrie
stare at each other in shock. Carrie rushes out.

We see the ensuing fight between Tim and Lisa. She gives
him back his key and, on the way out the door, says she hopes
his shrink can help him with his compulsive relationships
with women. Which reminds Tim all over again: Dr. Joslin is
dead. Despairing, he wants very much to get in touch with
Carrie but realizes he can't remember her last name because
he was drinking too much. He and his friend Lou try to summon up her name. They free-associate, and Tim almost
thinks he's remembered. "Carry Nation!" he exclaims. Then,
disheartened, he remembers, "No. That's someone else."

Meanwhile, Carry talks about Tim to her friend Claudia,
who currently waits tables at the hugest steakhouse in the
country, called the Singing Steer, which features a large ce-
ramic singing cow outside. Lonely and distraught and lacking
the nerve to call Tim up, Carrie is convinced by her father to

come for a visit. His name is RAY JAMISON, and he's a tall, elegant, melancholy man who lives in a nearby suburb. Father and daughter are very close. Carrie spends the night in her girlhood bedroom, surrounded by mementoes of her early life: Peter Frampton posters, a photo of herself and her beloved mother, who died when she was in high school.

Later, back in town, Carrie goes on a series of depressing dates with men who are wrong for her. Tim, meanwhile, has a series of pointless little flirtations with students, including a particularly provocative sophomore named LIZZIE GREER. He confides in Lou about how much he wishes he could see Carrie again. Late one night, Tim and Lou break into Dr. Joslin's office to go through his files and find Carrie's last name. As they look through the files, they come upon Tim's, which is exciting to read, and they are almost caught by a policeman cruising the area, but they manage to escape in time, though without finding Carrie's file.

Carrie is so forlorn over Dr. Joslin's death that she goes to a new therapist, a rather insane and overbearing, caftan-wearing woman, DR. LAZAR, who makes Carrie do something with percussion instruments and memories of her own birth. Carrie thinks this is ludicrous, and she flees mid-session. On the way out, she runs into . . . Tim, who has also been given Dr. Lazar's name. She encourages him to leave with her, and like guilty teenagers they run outside. They agree to meet the next day at a memorial service for Dr. Joslin, which they see an announcement for in the *Providence Journal*.

At the service, the other patients are there: mostly neurotic and sympathetic, with one or two who seem downright crazy, all paying tribute to their dead shrink. Then Dr. Joslin's wife, MIRIAM JOSLIN, speaks. She's lovely and dignified in a Claire Bloom kind of way, although totally grieving and in shock, talking painfully about the wonderful years she had with her husband. She quotes the Robert Louis Stevenson line: "Marriage is a long conversation." Everyone is very moved, especially Carrie and Tim, who feel deep stirrings for each other.

They go out to dinner on a real, formal date. They go to the Singing Steer, which Carrie picked, so that Claudia can check Tim out. The date goes well, and Claudia gives Carrie a thumbs-up sign. When Carrie goes to the ladies' room, though, Claudia comes over to Tim, pointing to a diagram of a cut-up cow on the menu. She says to him, "See this diagram? This is the sirloin. This is the rump. Basically, this is a picture of you with a cow's face if you ever hurt Carrie."

After dinner, Tim and Carrie walk to her apartment. It's tense, because they still have their particular problems that haven't been cured yet: she talks about her ex-boyfriend a few too many times, and he allows himself to flirt with a student who says hello to him on the street. At Carrie's house, they start to make out, when suddenly she smells something. Is it a fire? No. "It's like burning leaves," he says. "And . . . Froot Loops," she finishes. They see a burning ember in the dark across the living room, and then there's the sound of inhaling and the orange glow brightens, illuminating the face of Dr. Joslin, back from the dead.

Act Two

After much shrieking and the light being snapped on, Dr. Joslin finally calms them down (he's quite good at this) and explains. Yes, he says, he's truly a ghost who's been allowed to come back to earth to finish up a bit of unfinished business:

them. They're the only ones who can see him. He will help them with their individual problems if they agree not to sleep with each other. Based on their psychological profiles, they would be a disaster as a couple. In lieu of his usual fee, he says, he wants them to do him a favor. Sure, they agree, because in their stunned state they'll agree to anything.

He takes them to his house, a stately Victorian, where they secretly observe his sleeping wife, who has lots of balled-up Kleenex beside the bed and a copy of *Surviving the Death of a Loved One* lying on her night table. "Look after Miriam," he says. "Make sure she's okay; I can't stand how lonely she must be."

How can we look after her? they ask, but Dr. Joslin says it's up to them to figure it out. Then he puffs on his pipe and disappears. (The pipe is his conduit to and from the spirit world.) Carrie and Tim realize that they are in a stranger's bedroom in the middle of the night; Miriam starts to stir and then wakes up, thinking there's a burglar. They frantically sneak out of the house.

Dr. Joslin appears to each of them separately: to Tim as he's flirting with a student, and to Carrie as she sits looking at an old videotape of herself with her ex-boyfriend David. He bolsters their confidence and keeps them in line.

In return, Carrie and Tim decide to pose as journalists who have been given a grant from the Freudian Society to write a book about Dr. Joslin. Miriam Joslin gives them total access to her, because she loves talking about her late husband, showing slides of the couple when they were young: the time they saw a mouse, their honeymoon in Rome.

However, during the interviews she says some things that are painful for Dr. Joslin to hear (he's in the corner listening, moved by his own good deeds). Miriam reveals that she had an affair when they were young, because her husband, Miles, was always lost in his work.

Dr. Joslin is shaken by this. He storms off, and Carrie and Tim invent an excuse to Miriam so they can follow him. He walks down the street angrily, when suddenly they all notice a person on a window ledge, threatening to jump. A crowd has formed. Dr. Joslin rushes into the building, Carrie and Tim following behind. He goes up to the window and, using Carrie and Tim à la Cyrano, he talks the suicidal person down. We see the way he uses his brilliance and intuition and experience to find out what route to take in order to help this person. We also see Carrie and Tim working as a team, close together in a moment of intensity. They embrace with relief when the suicidal person is saved, and they want more than anything to kiss, but they refrain. They don't want to be screwed up forever; they want to follow Dr. Joslin's advice and get better.

The seasons change. It's winter in New England, and both Miriam and Carrie's father, Ray, are alone. Carrie and Tim decide to introduce these two lonely middle-aged people to each other. The foursome goes ice-skating at the Brown University rink, and Dr. Joslin struggles to keep up, gliding above the ice. He doesn't like the fact that Carrie's father, Ray, is hovering around Miriam. After the skating party, Dr. Joslin angrily reminds Carrie of all the negative things she's said about her father in therapy (how he had trouble holding down a job, how he never took the time to get to know her when she was young, how he was responsible for letting her pet hamster loose).

Maybe you should ask your father to leave, Tim whispers to her. She tells him no, her father wasn't doing anything wrong. They argue over how much they ought to be listening to Dr. Joslin in the first place. "He's the expert," Tim says. But Carrie feels that Dr. Joslin is blinded by his own strong feelings for his wife. He wants Miriam to be happy, but not *too* happy. For the first time in a long while, Carrie's father, Ray, seems cheered up. And Miriam, too, has come to life in Ray's presence. Dr. Joslin warns that unless Carrie removes her father from Miriam's life, Carrie and Tim will no longer receive Dr. Joslin's therapeutic services. This is a hard decision for Carrie, but she makes it: she says good-bye to her beloved shrink. "That's it?" Dr. Joslin says, astonished. "Yes," says Carrie. "That's it."

"Well," says Dr. Joslin angrily, "if that's the way you feel about it, then I'm leaving for good." He starts to puff on his pipe, but Tim begs him to stay. "*I* still need you!" cries Tim. "I'm a hopeless flirt! I'm irresponsible! I'm a big baby! I'll never settle down!"

But Dr. Joslin is gone in a cloud of smoke. Tim is very angry with Carrie for driving Dr. Joslin away. While Miriam and Ray start to have a relationship, Carrie and Tim stop speaking to each other entirely.

Act Three

Carrie goes home and we see her in her life, very lonely. No Tim, no Dr. Joslin. We also see Tim, who's equally lonely, hanging out with his friend Lou, moping. Finally in her loneliness Carrie calls her ex-boyfriend David up. They arrange a date at the Singing Steer. Tim, meanwhile, finally calls Lizzie, the particularly flirtatious student. He makes a date to see her for the same night, also at the Singing Steer.

The night arrives, and Carrie's friend Claudia, who is waiting on Carrie and David's table, is the first to see that

Tim and Lizzie are also here. She tries desperately to keep the couples apart. But finally Tim and Carrie meet and have a huge fight in the restaurant. Carrie mocks how young Lizzie is; Tim mocks the fact that Carrie has regressed and called her old boyfriend. Carrie throws a hanger steak at Tim. Everyone is appalled and embarrassed.

David goes home with Carrie. It's finally him; she's really got him back. But Claudia was right; he *is* boring. He sells coasters. And talks about them, too. Carrie misses Tim terribly. Finally she asks David to leave. Meanwhile, Tim is with Lizzie, and he misses Carrie as well. He doesn't want to touch Lizzie, but instead he drives her back to her dorm. She's furious with him for being such a tease. "Figure out what you want," she says as she slams the door. He does know what he wants—for the first time ever—and he decides to do something about it.

It's late night in Providence, Rhode Island. Carrie's in her house; she's inside alone, in her nightgown, watching a Victoria Principal infomercial. The buzzer rings. She goes to her front door and there, out in front of the house, is the cow from the Singing Steer. And then it begins to sing. It sings something like "I was an idiot, and I steered us the wrong way." Tim stands up; he's behind the cow. (He borrowed it from Claudia for an hour.) He and Carrie have a big moment of tenderness, realizing they need each other, that they want each other more than anything. Over the cow, they kiss.

They realize Dr. Joslin was wrong; they *are* good for each other. Their problems started to go away not by endlessly talking them through, but by living them out. They want to tell Dr. Joslin. "How can we find him?" Tim asks. They try to summon him, but he doesn't come.

"I know," says Carrie suddenly. "I know where he is

tonight." They return the cow and then go to the top of the Hilton, to the revolving restaurant where Miriam and Ray are having a date. They go up and find the older couple dancing together. Sure enough, Dr. Joslin is sitting at the bar, watching his wife in a darkly protective way and muttering jealously. They confront him, telling him that he has to let Miriam have a life. "She can't live her life in memory of you," Carrie says. "Look at her; it's the first time her eyes have shone since you died. She's herself again, the girl you married."

"Marriage *is* a long conversation," Tim says, quoting the line Miriam had read at the memorial service. "But even the best conversations have to end."

They remind him of many of the details from his marriage over the years. "What about all of that?" they say. "Would you have wanted it not to have happened?"

"No," he says softly, looking at his wife dancing with Ray. "No. You're both right." Then he looks at Carrie and Tim, his eyes narrowing. "And you two," he says—because he is extremely aware of subtle changes in people—"there's something different here. Something's changed."

"Yes," Tim tells him. "We've fallen in love." They're frightened of what he's going to say. They know he was against it. But he smiles slightly, as though he'd always planned it in some way. And he takes a copy of a small book from his breast pocket and hands it to them. It's called *Staying Together*, by Dr. Miles Joslin. Read the inscription, he says. "To Carrie and Tim," they read. "I hope you will be together forever. With affection, Miles Joslin." They realize that he *had* planned it all. They exclaim and try to show gratitude, but he waves them off, embarrassed. He says he's been hanging around too long as a ghost. "Freud did that, too," he confides. "Freud stayed around so long he watched the pilot episode of *Welcome Back, Kotter*. And Jung! He was doing the macarena!" Sad as it is, it's time to leave his wife to have her own life, and to leave Carrie and Tim to have theirs.

Fighting back tears, he starts to light his pipe. "Wait!" Carrie says. "Back in your office before your heart attack, you were about to tell me something about love. What was it?"

"Oh, that?" he says. "You've already found it out. That you have to be willing to let go. I think I forgot to do that myself." And he lights his pipe and disappears into a burst of smoke, letting go once and for all. The pipe drops to the floor; Carrie picks it up and holds it.

Carrie and Tim watch her father and Miriam dancing. Then they join the dancers in the revolving restaurant, whirling around the floor, getting on with their lives and finally able to fall in love.

Chapter Three

The Treatment and Its Elements

In broad strokes, here's the way *We Have to Stop* breaks down into three acts:

Act one: Introduction of Carrie and Tim and their separate brands of unhappiness. Introduction of Dr. Joslin. He dies, and Carrie and Tim meet. In their mutual despair, they start to have a relationship but are stopped by their unresolved problems. Dr. Joslin comes back from the dead and tells them he'll help them, if they help him.

Act two: Carrie and Tim start to fall in love. Carrie's father, Ray, meets Dr. Joslin's widow, Miriam, and they start to have a relationship. Dr. Joslin becomes meddlesome. He gives Carrie an ultimatum: either she keep Miriam away from Ray, or Dr. Joslin will leave Carrie and Tim. Carrie refuses to obey him. Dr. Joslin disappears again. And Tim, angry with Carrie, leaves her too.

Act three: Carrie is unhappy again, and Tim is too. Tim is filled with remorse and goes to win Carrie back. They kiss, then they want to show Dr. Joslin that they're in love. They find him watching Miriam and Ray and confront him. They help him "let go" of his life, just as he has helped them "let go" of their obstacles to love. The movie ends with the two couples—older and younger—dancing.

As you can see, the treatment has a conventional three-act structure, which can be dissected as follows:

- Act one introduces the *setup*, ending with what is known as a "plot point," something that takes the action in an entirely new direction.
- Act two is the *playing out* of that plot point, developing complications and conflicts, and ending on another plot point, and unresolved conflict.
- Act three, finally, is the *resolution* of that conflict.

It's fine to be flexible and try variations as you become more comfortable with the craft of writing both treatments and scripts, but for right now, as you begin the whole process, I would advise you to structure your story in a conventional fashion—even if it feels dull to you to do so. A predictable structure containing really interesting elements can create an excellent movie, one that has true shape to it.

If you have paid a lot of attention to theater, you may be a bit confused by the discussion of "acts" in this book. These acts aren't the same as the acts of a play, which tend to all be the same length. In the theater, it's perfectly acceptable to have a one-act, two-act or three-act play; Shakespeare's plays, of course, had *five* acts. All of these possibilities are acceptable and not seen as unusual. But there is no such thing as a one-act screenplay. (Well, maybe there is, but it's not going to get produced.)

A good friend of mine, screenwriter Mark Saltzman, thinks that most screenplays aren't really three-acters at all.

"I compare the screenplay form with a triptych," he says, referring to a type of three-paneled painting that was popular in earlier centuries. "There's a wing on either side of the center panel, but it's that crucial center panel—the so-called second act—that really tells the story."

This is an interesting way of looking at the form, and it's worth remembering that the term *act* has a different meaning in screenplay parlance than it does anywhere else. The "acts" are discrete units of your script that each serve a separate function; the bulk of your story will reside firmly in act two.

Some people are inclined to "name" each of the acts of a treatment or screenplay; doing so helps clarify what the thrust of each act actually is. In *We Have to Stop*, what would you name the individual acts? Act one might be called "Carrie and Tim are desperately unhappy and don't know how to be in love." Act two could be called "They start to learn how to be in love, but then they lose everything." And act three could be called "Now both Tim and Carrie learn what they didn't know and fall in love forever." Not exactly catchy titles, but they're only meant for the writer's eyes during the process of writing. They help you remember what you're trying to achieve. They help you keep in mind your imperative.

IMPERATIVE

Locating imperative is essential to writing a successful treatment and a successful screenplay. It keeps the story moving forward. There's a kind of Russian-nesting-doll simplicity to keeping the imperative in sight: First, you should determine the overarching description of the entire movie. Next, determine the theme of each act, and then "name" the acts accordingly. And then, going down to a more molecular level, you might even determine the imperative/theme of each *scene* within an act. This exercise may seem crazily microscopic and obsessive, and I suppose it is. (But most writers are obsessive.) And unlike novels, short stories, plays and feature articles, the screenplay works best when most aspects have been worked out thoroughly beforehand—and that includes the beginning, the middle and the end.

This is probably quite different from the way you've been taught to think about writing; in the past, you might have left a lot up to intuition, or what kind of mood you were in when you sat down at your computer, or how sentimental you were feeling at that particular moment. But now, regardless of mood, unless your script is carefully designed before you actually write it, it's unlikely to work.

When I first started writing in earnest as a teenager, I imagined an entire moral universe for my stories, and I made sure to punish my corrupt characters (drug dealers, plagiarists, crooked politicians) and reward the good ones (grandmothers, orphans, kindhearted prostitutes)—although sometimes I would tragically and senselessly punish the good ones in a shameless attempt to "move" my readers. (Luckily, the only readers I had at the time were those who had purchased my high-school literary magazine, and so not too many people were forced into submissive tears by my manipulative teenaged prose.) Adolescent writers often impose a moral structure on their beginning attempts at writing. Sometimes, however, they impose no structure at all, hoping to imitate the French existentialists they have just read in their lit class. Both approaches have serious problems.

John Gardner wrote eloquently about the difference between art and polemic: if you knew exactly where you were going in a work of fiction and also knew exactly how to get there, then what you were writing wasn't art at all, but polemic. For instance, consider an author of antiabortion pamphlets—screeds that start out by declaring something to the effect of "Abortion is murder, and here's why . . ." Then the pamphlet continues by showing the reader exactly *why* abortion is supposedly "murder," perhaps through detailed descriptions of what takes place on the fetal level throughout the first few months of pregnancy. By the time the pamphlet ends, the writer can say, in summation, "And so, as I've proven, *abortion is murder.*" There's a circularity to such an enterprise, a suspicious neatness. The writer sets out to make a specific point that he or she feels strongly about, and then spends the rest of the time expressing that point until it's been fully made, and then the polemic ends.

In "art," on the other hand, a writer may start out by saying the equivalent of "Abortion is murder. And here's why . . ." But the writer holds the possibility that this point isn't necessarily true, or at least not true in the way that he or she currently thinks. The writer leaves him or herself open to surprises, to new insight, to the possibility of an epiphany rising out of left field. The novel may not even remotely "prove" that abortion is murder. Through its characters and the sinuousness of its story and all its shades of subtlety, it may, in fact, reach the conclusion that abortion *isn't* murder. That it's a necessity. That it's a valid moral choice. The novel may, in the end, not even really be about abortion at all. If the writer leaves himself or herself open to the possibility of being informed by his or her own work and the associations that may be made during the process, then anything can happen. Which is, of course, one of the great pleasures of art.

A screenwriter falls somewhere between John Gardner's notion of a polemicist and an artist. A screenwriter needs to have the strong convictions of the polemicist, as well as a set of predetermined "arguments" for those convictions. But a screenwriter also needs to have the gracefulness to show the complexities of a situation, as well as the subtlety to develop not just the black-and-white areas but the gray ones, too. And since no polemicist has ever been able to create a three-dimensional character (read Ayn Rand's novels for a good example of this point), the artistic impulse will help the screenwriter make the characters seem real. Also, since no polemicist on earth has ever had a good sense of humor (Ayn Rand again), if you want to write funny, you'd better summon the artist within yourself.

CHARACTERS IN A TREATMENT

As you bring out each character in your treatment, you should give him or her a couple of telling details and characteristics. In *We Have to Stop*, I chose to mention Carrie's age, immediately giving the reader an inkling about casting considerations. Think about characters you've loved in novels; weren't you always able to picture them in your mind when you were reading the book? And wasn't it jarring and unpleasant when the movie version came along, and the actor playing the lead looked nothing like what you'd imagined (curvaceous and almost womanly Sue Lyon playing the supposedly unsophisticated Lolita in the original film)? Leave some latitude so that the part is castable, but do make the character more than a generic young person with "rugged good looks" or "a lithe, sensual appearance."

I wanted the reader to learn some facts about the characters right up front. About Carrie, I wanted the reader to know:

- She is an unhappy but charming woman.
- She doesn't feel sorry for herself.
- She is taking action to try to get over her problems.

This last point is a particularly important one. If movie audiences think a character is doing nothing to help herself, or that she merely feels sorry for herself, they will not respond very charitably toward her. Audiences treat characters as though they were real people. In my teaching experience, this is often true in beginning literature classes. I once taught Tillie Olsen's great short story "I Stand Here Ironing," about a mother looking back over her life, explaining why she made the choices she did, some of which hurt her daughter. I was taken aback when a freshman stood up in the middle of the class and announced that she couldn't keep reading the story because she had absolutely no sympathy for the narrator. "Why should I care about her?" she cried. "She's a terrible mother! She deserves what she gets!"

Of course, as I tried to explain in class that day, fictional characters aren't real people who need our punishment or praise. But it is true that they exist in a self-contained universe, observed so closely that their moral code is open to discussion. A character who actually *does something* about her situation—rather than simply being passive and letting things be done to her—not only projects a movie forward, but she also becomes a more sympathetic figure. Characters must change over the course of a movie, and we have to be able to track the arc of that change.

One way to help the reader of your treatment imagine the character better is by including fragments of dialogue. A treatment can feel as airless as an elevator, and I've found that introducing a small amount of dialogue reminds the reader (and the writer too) that this is a blueprint for something that will actually be said out loud.

MOOD AND SETTING IN A TREATMENT

After the central characters have all made their way into the treatment, there's room for you to fill out the environment of the movie: the sort of details that will give it a real sense of place as well as an essence, a feeling, an overriding mood. Describe the place and mood of a movie such as *Chinatown*. Free-associating, you might say "Los Angeles" and "sinister," but there's much more to be said. What about *Fargo*? It isn't just "Dakotan" or "wintry." *Mood* isn't simply produced by fog machines swirling on a moor; it's comprised of the small things, too. In *We Have to Stop*, I wanted to lock the New England city of Providence, Rhode Island, into winter, with its attendant possibilities of bleakness, if you're alone, or coziness, if you're in love. Showing the characters out and about—ice-skating at the university rink, for instance, a detail that would take up only a brief moment of screen time— gives the reader a specific, as opposed to generic, understanding of the contained universe of this movie.

If you were to have a creativity mantra in mind while writing a screen treatment, whether the treatment is meant for your eyes only or someone else's, it ought to be "specific, not generic." The more details you give us, and the more idiosyncratic and interesting those details are, the more your movie will be your own. You can find your "voice"—a word that gets bandied about a lot in Hollywood—through the accretion of details in a treatment. It's much easier to find your voice now, while writing the treatment, than it will be later on. If you don't have a strong and distinctive voice by the time you've begun work on the script, it will be tough to find it at all.

FASHIONING YOUR OWN TREATMENT

Let's say that you are intent on writing the Brooklyn girlhood movie called *Bay Parkway*. You've thought it out, examining motives, character arcs, locale and secondary characters. Now you feel it's time to start writing the treatment.

The first question you ought to ask yourself, as you sit down to fashion your treatment, is this: *What's the overarching description of this movie?* When you think you know what it is, write it down. Perhaps you write: "This is a movie about a young girl growing up in Brooklyn during World War II, whose life is forever changed by the war."

Or you might get slightly more specific: "This is a drama about a young girl coming of age in Brooklyn during World War II—and how the war changes her hopes for herself, her family, and her definition of love."

Or else you might focus on character: "This is a coming-of-age movie set in Brooklyn during World War II, centering on an overprotected, sensitive eleven-year-old girl who becomes aware of the effects of war, which bring her into the real world for the first time."

You don't have to give away much up front, but a little taste of what sort of movie this will be is always welcome. Next, you might describe the setting. Such as: "Brooklyn in 1940 is a place of vigilance and hand-wringing and hopefulness, in which entire neighborhoods are bound together by a war taking place across an ocean."

Or: "Brooklyn during World War II is filled with candy stores, crowded subway trains, and apartment houses with worried people in every window. But it's also filled with noise and light and the Andrews Sisters and the slapping-down of cards at Saturday-night canasta games."

However you describe your setting, do so in a way that is evocative and specific. As in fiction, there are some adjectives that do nobody any good because they are generic and just lie there flatly on the page. The idiosyncratic writing teacher, editor and fiction zealot Gordon Lish used to tell his students never to use the words "thighs" or "restaurant" in a story (don't ask me why). My list of what not to put in a treatment isn't quite so cryptic. My verboten words to describe a setting include: "nice," "pretty," and "creepy," among others. There are similarly unhelpful words to describe characters, such as "sad," "angry," and "mean." All these words share a dull vagueness.

Suppose you want to describe one of the secondary characters in *Bay Parkway*, a teenaged friend of the protagonist, named JOYCE KELLMAN. At first you say of her, "Joyce is kind and generous with herself and always trying to please others." But then you read this over and think to yourself that the description is vague. It doesn't help you to visualize the character. Is there a way to make it better? Try to think about the way you might describe someone in a short story, play or article. Would you ever settle for calling her "kind and generous"? (I hope the answer is no.)

You need to write as well in a screenplay as you do in all other forms of writing. Therefore, that line of description might be changed to read something like: "Wherever Joyce goes, men turn and stare—not that she notices; her knitting needles are always rapidly clicking away as she knits sweaters for soldiers, and she's always preoccupied by her efforts."

I'm not suggesting that this alternative description is an example of good writing, only that it follows the specificity rule. It allows you to visualize Joyce; when you see her now, you see a beautiful girl surrounded by lengths of wool, and you hear the clicking of her needles. You witness her in action, rather than static and frozen, as if in a Madame Tussaud tableau.

Action is the most important factor to think about when developing a character. The things people *do* in a movie tell us who they are; in a novel or piece of journalism, the way people think or talk tells us a great deal about them, but if you rely heavily on talk in a script, your movie will be talky.

Your treatment should, accordingly, be impelled by action, which is the best vehicle for explicating a character and having him or her undergo change. Showing characters in action gives the reader a sense of the larger world of the movie. *A character never exists in isolation.* When you describe someone in a treatment, never forget who he or she is in relation to the other characters and the environment they all inhabit.

Next, on to your story. A treatment can literally map out every scene in the movie, or merely every pivotal scene and a few of the less pivotal but still important ones. (Sometimes a lesser scene might be included in a treatment because it illustrates a central conflict, or introduces one of the other characters.)

As you write, keep in mind the "names" that you've given your acts. If one of the scenes that you're describing doesn't further the theme of the act, then take it out. This can be a difficult lesson for writers to learn; many of us have come to think that our actual writing is the most important element in the mix, and that if a scene is extremely well written its existence is justified, even if nothing actually happens in the scene to further the story.

This is not true when writing a movie. Remember Richard Price's distinction between the "language" of fiction and the story "momentum" of a screenplay? I'm not suggesting that you shouldn't be besotted with language now—you *should*—but you should *never* use an atomized mist of gorgeous or staccato or just plain idiosyncratic language to replace movement in a story, or even to try and disguise the fact that your story is weak. A scene that does not further the theme of your act weighs down your treatment; if you were to shoot such a scene in the movie, it would eventually find its way to the cutting-room floor.

Be sure to delineate—if only for yourself—the places where your acts break. Your first act ought to set up the imperative—introducing the major characters and their general situation, and ending with the plot point that reveals their predicament. To illustrate this plot point in the treatment, you might give a few lines of dialogue from the crucial scene (or scenes) that ends the act.

Act two is the longest and most detailed of your three acts; it's the heart and soul of your story. This act is over only when *all* the important elements and characters have been explored, the central conflict(s) thoroughly investigated, and a new plot point introduced that sends the story into a spin and creates a sense of chaos. I'm using the word *chaos* in its loosest sense here, to imply not that there's necessarily hysteria onscreen, with people screaming and crying and carrying on, but that the plot point has created a *disorder*—an imbalance, a dissatisfaction, an unnaturalness of some sort, involving the central plot or the emotional concerns of the characters—that needs to be resolved, one way or another, by the end of act three.

The third act is sweeping-up time. It's a relatively short act that restores the elements to their "natural" state. (I don't mean that life will return to the way it was at the beginning of the movie; instead, some sort of new state is usually achieved.) Any major unhappiness on the part of a character is resolved or at least fully examined and understood. Characters finally know where they stand with each other. A nebulous situation is clarified. All may not be sweetness and light and snuggly cuddling by the end of the movie—in fact, your protagonists may fly off a cliff à la *Thelma and Louise*—but usually, by the time the final credits roll, changes have taken place both in the story and in the characters, and everything has been revealed.

Because you're already a writer, your treatment will read more cleanly than most treatments anyone reads in Hollywood. Create a longer version for yourself and, if necessary, a much shorter one to show others. Your treatment stands a good chance of being witty and specific and interesting, because you probably know how to capture those qualities in your work. As far as its structual soundness is concerned, that's something that you'll develop a feel for as you go along. Like all other types of writing, it gets easier with practice.

I'm aware that this chapter has saddled you with an enormous amount of delayed gratification, when all you really want to do is get going on the script. But writing a good treatment first is going to provide you with the equipment you'll need when you actually get started.

Chapter Four

Page One

For many writers, the best part of the writing process is the very beginning, before we are damned by our own imperfect words. In the moments following the gathering of ideas and prior to actually putting them down on paper, it seems as though anything is possible. We might be brilliant; we might write a screenplay that would make the gods at Miramax weep. A little bit of hubris is a good thing; it can actually enhance writing. I usually gather various snack foods around me when I'm beginning something, knowing that I'll be there for a while and will need sustenance, but also because I want to give myself a little illicit treat to mark the pleasurable starting moments of a new project. When I begin writing, I like to feel happy but disciplined; the goal is a contented Zenlike state achieved through small indulgences, good ideas and big fantasies. But it's best not to linger *too* long in fantasy; the real work to be done is massive. It's always a good idea to try to actualize the ideas before they sour, or even disappear.

Someone once said that the shelf life of most books is somewhere between yogurt and cottage cheese, and I think the same is true of ideas. If you talk them to death or tell yourself that you're going to start writing one of these days, but the days just keep passing, then you are in danger of losing your momentum.

Writers occasionally worry that creating an elaborate treatment before getting to work on the screenplay puts them in danger of losing their momentum, but this isn't so. A good treatment ensures that you never forget your goals or your design for achieving them; essentially, it reminds you of the way to write your script.

When you've got your treatment in hand, you should purchase the appropriate screenwriting software for your computer. I don't mean the kind that purports to help you actually structure and shape the script and come up with ideas and characters for it (such as Dramatica Pro, which some people swear by, especially during the rewriting phase), but rather the kind that formats for you as you go along. A good program gives you shortcuts, indenting or capitalizing for you so you can focus on the ideas rather than the busy-work. There are several programs on the market; I use Final Draft, and it was easy to get accustomed to.

It's very important that you find concentrated time in which to write your script. Ideally, this would be at least two hours a day, taking into account your other work, since many writers have jobs or other projects they need to be working on—projects that actually give them an income and don't need to be written on "spec." If you were a beginning novelist, I would never tell you that working on your book for two hours a day would suffice. But screenplays are different from novels; they are often more formulaic, and they don't require you to sacrifice your entire tortured soul or throw yourself on the grave of Tolstoy. But they do require:

- a well-thought-out treatment
- attention to the demands of structure
- concentrated time each day to work
- a quiet workplace

When you actually begin writing, you'll find yourself either fevered and inspired and able to write fast and furiously, or else you'll be at somewhat of a loss, as many writers are at the start. If you've managed to find a quiet place and a few hours of uninterrupted time, but somehow when you start page one of the script the words just don't come, try to figure out whether the problem originates in the idea (treatment) or the execution (script). Then try to solve the problem as logically as you can, making the appropriate changes in the script and/or treatment. Keep working on the opening until you have one scene or sequence of scenes that you like well enough. Then go back and take another look at that opening, asking yourself whether it sets the tone that you originally meant to set, and whether it foreshadows the situation that you plan to create. If it does both, then stop tinkering for now, and keep going forward.

I'm all for endurance in screenwriting; the longer the stretches of writing you can generate, the better. There will be plenty of time for rewriting later. Right now, if the thoughts and ideas are in place (not to mention the arc of the characters and the plot), then by all means, gather pages.

Volume is important; I know of writers who spend a lot of time agonizing over small moments in their scripts, getting bogged down in the details as though they were painting Fabergé eggs for the czar. If you spend that kind of time on your script right now, you will not be true to the spirit of screenwriting, which is often about big, bold strokes, about movement. Learning to move forward as you write will help keep that idea in mind. The *action* should be constant; this isn't a pointillist painting you're creating. So if everything seems to be working, by all means go full speed ahead.

Something else that all screenwriters need to do constantly at the beginning stages of writing is to read other people's scripts. This helps familiarize you with not only the structure of screenplays but also the mechanics of them, too, the ins and outs of "EXT. PATIO — DAY" and "DISSOLVE TO:" I'll deal a little bit in this chapter with the "vocabulary" common to all scripts, but you will get a real crash course simply by reading as many scripts as you can. There are plenty of published screenplays available in the bookstore; better yet, get hold of some actual unpublished ones that circulate over the Internet, or that show up for sale on street corners (my friend Peter used to get all his scripts from a sidewalk vendor in Brooklyn) or else through a friend who works in film. In addition, check out *Scenario* magazine, which publishes entire scripts of recent movies.

Familiarizing yourself with the way a script reads and feels is enormously helpful. A published screenplay tends to be seamless; it's usually what's known as a "shooting script"—the version that finally, after dozens of different-colored drafts and multiple cuts and changes, went before the cameras. An unpublished screenplay, on the other hand, tends to be in rougher, still-evolving shape. I was recently given a copy of the script *Good Will Hunting*, which turned out to be very different from the version I had seen in the theater. The rough-edged screenplay is a valuable tool; if you can find two different drafts of the same movie, you'll get an idea of the process the writer went through and the choices he or she made (whether under duress from a studio or not), which may one day be useful to you when you have to make similar choices.

I thought I'd show you the first two pages, annotated, of my screenplay *Surrender, Dorothy*, based on my novel of that same name. It's not that I hold these pages up as a paragon of screenwriting, but they're real, they're mine, and I can explain why I made the decisions I did. Through looking at these pages, you can familiarize yourself with the fairly inflexible format and lingo of the screenplay.

```
FADE IN:
An answering machine

A telephone RINGS. Then there's a CLICK, and
the spools of a cassette tape in the machine
begin to turn, as the recorded message be-
gins to play.
                    NATALIE (O.S.)
            Hi, it's Natalie here!

And we pull back to reveal:


1. INT. NATALIE'S KITCHEN — DAY

2. A  big,  sunny,  well-stocked  suburban
   kitchen.  A  Sub-Zero  refrigerator  with
   various  fruit-shaped  magnets  on  it—many
   of them holding up snapshots of the same
   pretty  girl  at  various  stages  of  her
   life, ranging from babyhood to her early
   twenties. At this last, grown-up stage,
   she is sexy, wry, simply beautiful.


3.                  NATALIE (O.S.)
4.     I'm  either  at  work,  in  the
       shower,  or  at  a  sale  at  Neiman
       Marcus. Leave a message!
```

5. The machine BEEPS as we zero in on one photo. A pineapple magnet holds up this picture of the young woman sitting with her arm around a pretty older woman. Mother and daughter.

Now we hear:

> SARA (O.S.)
> Hey, Mom, are you there? "Surrender, Dorothy!" I hope you're not having sex with some loser. Listen, I'm leaving for the house and I wanted to say good-bye. See you after Labor Day!

There is a CLICK as the telephone is hung up.

CUT TO:
6. Another answering machine

An ashtray sits on top of it, full of dead cigarette butts. A telephone begins to RING. The machine picks up with a CLICK, and the cassette spools begin to turn. We hear the following recorded message:

> SARA (O.S.)
> Hey there, this is Sara.

Now there is a fragment of raucous grunge MUSIC.

> SARA (O.S.)
> And this is the beep.

There is a long BEEP, and we pull back to reveal:

INT. SARA'S APARTMENT — EVENING

A young woman's apartment, filled with books,
CDs, cigarette boxes, magazines, makeup,
clothes, old stuffed animals — including
an ancient, one-eyed bunny. A framed photo
rests on an orange crate, showing a cluster
of college friends in caps and gowns. Smack
in the center of the cluster is the daughter from the photos in the last scene.

                    NATALIE (O.S.)
         Sara, are you home? (Beat) "Sur-
         render, Dorothy!" Oh, dammit, I
         missed you, kiddo. Well, too bad.
         It so happens your old mom does
         have a date. I'll tell you about
         it later. Drive carefully. And
         don't forget: eat nectarines,
         dear. But only <u>before</u> carbohy-
         drates. I read an article about it!

INT. FOYER — NIGHT

The darkened front hallway of Natalie's
house. The front door swings open and in
walk NATALIE SWERDLOW and HARVEY WISE. It's
dark, and we can't see them well. They are
two shadowy forms GIGGLING together and
groping each other.

                    HARVEY
         God, Natalie, you feel so good.

He backs her against a wall.

                    NATALIE
          Harvey, my L'Eggs.

                    HARVEY
          What's with your legs?

                    NATALIE
          Not legs. L'Eggs.

                    HARVEY
          What?

                    NATALIE
          My   panty   hose.   You're   ripping
          them.

(#1) At the opening of *Surrender, Dorothy* we have what's known as the *slug line,* the always-capitalized orientation in space that comes at the top of every new scene, either indicating an interior setting (INT.) or an exterior setting (EXT.) as well as an orientation in time (DAY, NIGHT, AFTERNOON, IMMEDIATELY, AT THE SAME TIME, MOMENTS LATER, etc.)

A double-spaced line below that is (#2) the *description,* which could refer to what a room looks like, or what a character looks like or is doing, or some other description or action that's taking place onscreen. This should not take up more than a line or two.

As each *character* is introduced (#3)—always in capital letters at the initial introduction, and always in caps when he or she is speaking, then written regularly with every subsequent, descriptive appearance—an extremely brief but telling description is helpful. As with much else you'll be doing, you can lift part of this description right out of your treatment. If the character is not actually onscreen at this moment, his or her name is followed by an indication that the dialogue is being spoken offscreen (OS). If the character is speaking in a voice-over (VO) then this too should be noted.

Next we move on to the *dialogue* (#4), which is indented and falls directly beneath the character name. All significant *sound effects* (#5) are written in capital letters. Sometimes a writer chooses to capitalize a punctuated action, too. For instance, a line might read, "We see ten-year-old JAKE—slender, athletic—SLIDING smoothly into home plate." It's your choice; it just depends on how much you want to emphasize the action.

When making a segue between scenes (#6), you may choose to indicate the *transition* (CUT TO:, DISSOLVE TO:, FADE TO:, etc.). This isn't usually necessary, because it's clear to the reader that when one scene ends, we automatically "cut" to another locale. But if the segue is a particularly crisp, pointed, emphatic one, then CUT TO: might be warranted. On the other hand, a slow, thoughtful transition might be indicated by DISSOLVE TO: or FADE TO:. I'm reminded of the use of adverbs in fiction and journalism; I always tell students to use them with extreme economy—almost stinginess. My instinct about these transition phrases between scenes is the same: use them sparingly. Overuse can make them seem gratuitous.

Those are the basics for making a screenplay look professional. One of the more unprofessional things a beginning writer can do in a script is to include "camera instructions," essentially showing the director how to do his or her job. Although there are instances where this may be acceptable and even essential, indicating camera shots usually makes you seem amateurish; leave them out. As you become more experienced you'll find that giving some camera instructions—reverse angles, etc.—may be appropriate, but a good script shouldn't rely on complicated directions to convey itself. For now just stick to the essentials and lay out the setting and the characters and the story.

THE OPENING

The opening of a movie is a critical moment. If you don't grab the moviegoer right away, you probably never will. The opening should be extremely absorbing and irresistibly watchable. But it also should do at least one of the following:

- Illustrate an entire world in miniature
- Present an ongoing situation
- Show us a typical moment between central characters
- Establish a mood
- Foreshadow the central conflict of the screenplay
- Be part of a longer "sequence" of scenes that presents one of the themes of the movie. (For more on this point, see page 91.)

The opening should always be something that people will remember; it should never be merely a random moment in the middle of a scene. There needs to be a real reason that we are eavesdropping on the scene right now, as opposed to five minutes earlier. Nothing in your script should ever be random; pleasurable though it is just to hang out with intriguing characters, there must be an actual purpose to every scene, and this is especially crucial at the beginning of a movie.

Think about great first lines of books you've read. While you probably can't quote too many lines from *A Tale of Two Cities* offhand, you know that the opening is "It was the best of times, it was the worst of times." That line stands on its own and also serves as a miniature version of one of Dickens's themes. In a movie, the equivalent of a memorable literary opening line does not generally take the form of spoken words. It tends to be a visual image or series of images that is arresting and memorable and, of course, representative of the movie and its imperative.

Think of the opening of *Jaws*, in which a calm and beatific ocean swim becomes a sudden nightmare. Or the opening of *The Godfather*, in which an Italian immigrant nervously and humbly beseeches Don Corleone to help him knock someone off; the scene is dim, dark, and we keep pulling back and back until the formidable figure of Marlon Brando is revealed. Or the opening of *The Player*, one long unbroken shot that reveals the gestalt of an entire movie studio. I can't emphasize enough that the opening pages of your script will set the tone of the entire enterprise. If you do not write a terrific and representative beginning, you'll lose your reader very quickly.

The opening of my script *Surrender, Dorothy* is slightly unsettling, in that we don't actually see anyone onscreen. We hear a telephone ringing and then we hear a woman's voice, and all we see are the wheels of an answering machine turning. This is then counterpointed by a second telephone and a second answering machine. Why don't we *see* the women talking? Wouldn't it give us a stronger sense of these characters if we saw them sitting and dialing, and got a good look at their faces and how they dressed, and perhaps a few other small, revealing details such as the way they sat, or jiggled a leg, or held a drink? And wouldn't it be more dramatically interesting to have us see them in conversation—actually able to reach each other instead of talking into the frustrating dead air of an answering machine?

I had to consider all these questions, and make choices about them. Writing a script—even one based on a treatment—involves making plenty of critical decisions as you go along. It's sort of like one of those *Choose Your Own Adventure* books that my son reads; if you go off in one direction, everything will be different than it would have been if you had gone off in another direction. My instinct, in the opening moments of the script, was to show a mother-daughter relationship in the most distilled, concentrated way I could.

In the novel version, the relationship between Sara and her mother, Natalie, is shown very briefly, mostly in flashback. We do see them talking on the phone to each other, and we understand right away that the telephone is their lifeline. So when I started writing the script, I wanted to be true to the spirit of the novel as well as to find some concentrated way to make the relationship immediately understandable.

There was something else at work, too: I didn't want to show Sara, the daughter, onscreen, for reasons I will explain later. I already knew that the telephone would play a big role in the lives of this mother and daughter, so why not just have them leave messages on each other's machine? Telephone tag is a way of life at the end of the twentieth century, and I knew that voices speaking into answering machines instead of to actual people would resonate with an audience. Also, it would keep the audience wanting more, wanting to see what these women look like and who they are, and knowing that they might get a chance to do that if they kept watching.

But even beyond that, I also wanted to open with something memorable. I wanted a *device*. This is a word I often use when teaching writing, and sometimes I mean it to have a negative connotation, other times not. I believe that the best writing of all types employs "devices" of one sort or another; sometimes those devices feel cheap or unearned, and as a result the reader resents the writer and feels taken for a ride. When this is the case, though, the "device" is really more of a "gimmick." But in the right hands, a device can be enormously useful. It makes a vague scene specific, giving the reader an actual "thing" to focus on.

Movie devices need to be visual. What we retain most from movies is not the language we hear, but what we see. Remember the floating feather in *Forrest Gump* (whether you found that movie annoying or wonderful)? It appeared right at the start of the film, and it served as a device that gently led the viewer into the story, burnishing the edges of it with a quality of magic realism—a quality that remained central to the rest of the film. Your device might be found through an understanding of your characters, which was the way I stumbled upon the opening of *Surrender, Dorothy*. If you have a deep and specific knowledge of your characters—their foibles, particular strengths, idiosyncrasies, longings—you will be able to find an opening that shows your characters in a representative moment, if you so choose. (For more on character, see chapter 6.)

Alfred Hitchcock, who often used objects in an important, representative way in his films, opened *Strangers on a Train* by following two different sets of shoes—one belonging to a regular guy, one belonging to a "swell"—as they head toward each other through a train station and onto a train, eventually "meeting" as the shoes bump up against one another under a table in a train compartment. Only then do we get to know the owners of those shoes.

Another device might involve the setting; you could use your surroundings, in effect, to help you develop a relevant opening. (Think of the moors in *Wuthering Heights* and how central they are to the story, or of Manderley in *Rebecca*.)

Finally, if there's an object or action that will become the centerpiece of the movie later on, it might be a good idea to open the movie with that idea, before it's taken on the meaning that it will have later on (Rosebud from *Citizen Kane*, for example).

At this point these choices are entirely up to you. The way in which a writer comes upon an opening image or scene for a film is very individualized. But the effect needs to be not only strong, but also representatively so. It should also indicate genre. If this is a mystery, then the beginning of the movie should have an unsettling feel to it. If it's a comedy, let it be funny right away. And better yet, let the humor come not out of some sort of generic, observational, stand-up world view, but out of the characters and their situation (*Broadcast News*, *Annie Hall*).

FLASHBACKS

Remember the opening of *Terms of Endearment*, when Shirley MacLaine's character, Aurora Greenway, as a young mother is so neurotically worried that her infant, who's asleep in the crib, isn't breathing that she pinches her awake? Only when the baby screams and screams inconsolably is Aurora satisfied. This was a perfect setup for the movie. James L. Brooks used the device of the *flashback* to introduce the life-long craziness of the mother and the primary relationship of the film, which is between mother and daughter. When we flash-forward to the present day, we see the adult manifestations of that early interaction, and we realize that, essentially (as it is between ourselves and our own mothers), nothing has changed.

The same is true for *Beaches*, when Bette Midler's and Barbara Hershey's characters meet as little girls. The way they deal with each other becomes cemented forever, and added to this is the visual joke of seeing Mayim Biyalik, with her huge mass of red hair and charmingly *jolie-laide* face, doing an uncanny young Bette.

The flashback is a way to instruct audiences about the origins of the story and the characters. It shows the planting of a "seed," such as the opening of *Halloween*, in which the genesis of a murderer is shown in a shocking and violent childhood scene. In *The Devil's Own*, in which Brad Pitt plays an unrepentant IRA terrorist, a flashback at the beginning shows his character as a child witnessing the politically motivated murder of his father. This scene is meant to give us a "reason" for the terrorist politics of Pitt's character when he grows up.

My advice to you about using flashbacks at the opening of a film (or even elsewhere within the film) is to be very careful when you do so. The genesis of political convictions or murderous rage is difficult to explain in one quick scene— and flashbacks should *always* be quick, probably no more than a page or two. They work best not when explaining the origins of complex ideology but, rather, when outlining the origins of:

- relationships between characters
- an obsession of a character
- some piece of a mystery that will be unraveled over the course of the story

Billy Wilder often used flashbacks in a crucial way in his films; *Sunset Boulevard* is famously "narrated" by a dead man in a swimming pool (William Holden). *Double Indemnity* is narrated by murderous insurance salesman Walter Neff (Fred MacMurray), who gives his confession into a tape recorder. The flashback is entered through his narration. In both of these cases, the *entire movie* is a flashback. If you can pull off such a stunt in a screenplay, that's wonderful; flashbacks are always tricky, though, whether they take up the entire movie or just a few seconds, and they need to be handled with a great deal of control.

Sometimes flashbacks can serve a screenplay well. They can "bookend" an entire movie, providing a memorable opening and ending. This can structurally anchor a screenplay, but there needs to be a definite reason to use the device. Done poorly or unnecessarily, flashbacks can be an embarrassment, so use them carefully and sparingly. (In *Surrender, Dorothy*, although I'd put them in the novel, in the screenplay I did everything I could to avoid them.) If you find yourself using several of them in one movie, it may mean that you haven't found a way to explain enough through present-day action, dialogue and character, and it may be time to go back and correct these deficiencies.

VOICE-OVERS

Another device used at the opening of a screenplay is a *voice-over* (*Mildred Pierce*, *All About Eve*, many Woody Allen movies). This too is tricky, and when done badly it only points out the weaknesses of the movie. (Sometimes, when a movie is considered something of a mess after it's been shot, a director will add a voice-over in an effort to fortify the movie by giving it a stronger, more literal "voice." But if the voice isn't already in your movie, then you can't really put it in through voice-overs.) Look at *Annie Hall*, and *Manhattan*, in which the voice-over device is used liberally. This works well, because it isn't a substitute for voice but merely an amplification of a voice that we're already familiar with. Back when these movies were made, long before the Mia Farrow–Soon Yi mess, Woody Allen the *auteur* was indistinguishable from Woody Allen the character, and both were crankily lovable and charming. Allen knew he could use voice-overs because as soon as his actual voice began to speak, audiences paid attention and even began to laugh before he'd actually said something funny. The familiar voice of Woody Allen has almost as much resonance as if it were a visual image.

But most of the time, voice-overs do not have the same impact as a visual image. They can have the undesired effect of being maudlin and sentimental. (Think of *Love Story*, with Ryan O'Neal intoning the words of the novel.) It can be disorienting suddenly to hear the voice of a character we've neither met nor seen in action. A voice-over must always be accompanied by an appropriate visual—something compelling and relevant.

The movie *The Prince of Tides* relied on voice-overs. Like

Love Story, as well as *The Bridges of Madison County*, *The Age of Innocence* and *The Wings of the Dove*, *The Prince of Tides* was based on a famous novel. The director, Barbra Streisand, assumed (rightly, I think) that viewers would want to hear actual lines from the Pat Conroy novel many of them loved so much. It may be too awkward to put those lines in the mouths of characters as they talk to one another; voice-over takes care of that potential problem. In *The Prince of Tides*, an overblown but bizarrely compelling movie, the voice-overs let fans of the book feel like this was old-home week, and also gave this unwieldy movie a bit of shape. You should use voice-overs only if they add resonance or structure to your script. If they don't add either of these things, they may only annoy the audience.

A REMINDER ABOUT IMPERATIVES

This is a good time to take a look at your treatment and give yourself a refresher course in the imperatives of your script. If your screenplay is going to be character-driven, then by all means start the film with a moment of pure, undiluted character. This might mean showing a particular idiosyncrasy of one or more of the characters, or it might mean showing the way the characters speak to each other, particularly if their relationship is rife with conflict that is central to the story.

If a film opens in the wrong way, you'll know it. Most movies seek their own levels; if you've established to your satisfaction what is *driving* this movie, where its central energies lie—and you should have done this in your treatment—then your opening should be an outgrowth of that understanding. If you have a prolonged sequence either at or right near the opening (the wedding in *The Godfather*, the studio traveling shot in *The Player*), then the energies and drives of the movie will be amplified and expanded upon in that sequence.

If you're trying to write a moody, visual film that relies heavily on locale, use some of that locale to anchor the opening. One caveat here, though: I've often heard writers speak about how the locale is the main "character" in their screenplay or novel. According to them, an entire town can be a character, and so can a mountain, or a lake or the seashore. I understand their point—the environment of a film or a novel *is* highly important, and often readers or viewers leave the experience feeling as though they've been immersed in that environment and know it well, perhaps as well as they know the human characters. But I worry that such thinking has become something of a cliché and, worse, an easy escape route for writers to take when they're afraid that their characters aren't as fully realized as they ought to be.

Your setting is of great importance, and even though it may be as much a part of the screenplay as any other element, never let it eclipse your characters or the story. Some films are beautiful to look at and fairly anemic in all other aspects. (It's a syndrome that I call Barry Lyndonitis.) While there might be an audience for lovely, windswept, otherwise empty movies, I don't have much patience for them. "Movies," as their names imply, have to really *move*. And they never move on their own; the screenwriters have to push them.

Finally, when you're thinking about how to open your screenplay, you'll inevitably come to the question of tone. A comedy should, of course, be very, very funny from its opening moments. This might mean there's an antic humor that is charming and offhand and which we experience immediately, or else it might mean that the writer sets up an elaborate joke of some sort (usually a visual one) that takes a full scene to be revealed as a joke. While a comedy needs to be funny from the start (audiences are very unforgiving when they expect to be amused; ask any comedian who's been heckled in the first five minutes of his act, before he or she has had time to really loosen up), the reverse is not true. A sad movie does not have to be sad right away. In fact, it might be best if it isn't sad right away. Unlike humor, pathos is not usually revealed in short, quick bursts. If a character dies, for instance, the event isn't "sad" unless we've really gotten to know this character, and that knowledge can only take place over time, developed slowly in some dark cheese-cellar of emotion. There are, of course, exceptions to this rule, and one of them seems to be, on the surface, the children–and–small animals rule—by which I mean, if you kill off children or small animals before we've gotten to know them, the audience will still cry. But they aren't crying because they're sad, or because the screenwriter has done anything special. They're probably crying because it's a cheap trick and they're falling for it. If you want to create a genuine emotional effect, then you need to let the movie and its characters distill. Authentic emotion is hard-won, both in life and in the movies. (Bambi's mother didn't die until we'd gotten to know Bambi.)

Movies don't only divide up into funny and sad. There are plenty of other tones that describe them, and genres into which they fall. But in most of these instances, if you know the type of movie you're writing, you will be able to summon up the right sort of beginning. It goes without saying that a mystery will be somewhat suspenseful or unnerving, or that an innocent setup will be revealed as something much less innocent later on. A drama will be dramatic; a farce will be farcical. Finding the embodiments of these qualities—the essence of them—is the screenwriter's task. A writer with some previous experience has an advantage here.

Let's try to come up with an opening for our imaginary period-piece movie, *Bay Parkway*. We'll start with an image of a young girl riding an elevated train in Brooklyn, the sort of train that isn't around anymore, with yellow wicker seats, ceiling fans, and ads for Juicy Fruit gum and Ipana toothpaste on the walls, and businessmen fanning themselves with their dark felt hats.

We see the girl sitting squeezed between a businessman and a fat woman fanning herself with a newspaper. The girl is reading a screen magazine, perhaps with Clark Gable on the cover. So right away, from certain visual cues, we know when the movie takes place. And perhaps we hear a voice-over, in which the girl says, "It was a very different time, that summer. It was a time when men wore hats. And women swooned over Clark Gable. And I got my first training bra." Now there's a beat, and we see the newspaper that the fat woman is fanning herself with, and we can make out part of the headline, perhaps something about Hitler. And then the voice of the girl continues, with "And we had gone to war." Then we immediately cut away to a traveling shot of the train heading across the bridge into Brooklyn, and we see an expansive sweep of the city skyline, circa the early 1940s. And the credits roll.

Whether that opening is wildly inspired or not (okay, it's

not), it feels like an opening. And it does so for the following reasons:

- It is visual.
- It orients us in time and space.
- It introduces us to one of the central characters.
- It's in some way representative of the script as a whole.
- It sets a definite mood.

But the opening moments of this screenplay or any other aren't just there to be a microcosm of the movie as a whole, or even an advertisement for it. The opening can't just stand in isolation; it needs to provide a way into the rest of the movie. If you come up with a wonderful first scene or prolonged opening sequence but have no idea how to get from there to the rest of your movie, the wonderful scene or sequence may not be right. (I've spent far too much time trying hard to jam well-written but, in context, inappropriate or unnecessary scenes into my work, and I'd like to save you from such fruitless tasks.) Regardless of the device you use and whether the first few pages are hysterically funny or jarring or driven by the characters or their setting, the opening should always be an inviting doorway into the rest of your screenplay.

Chapter Five

Essentials: Scenes, Sequences, Subplots and Plot Points

As you start working on your script every day and feeling more comfortable gathering scene after scene, you may feel that you've been spoiled by your previous prose experiences. Whereas in the past you were allowed plenty of latitude, you now need to be a love-slave to structure, both within each scene and within the overarching script. To write a good scene, to commit it to paper, requires discipline and the distillation of ideas down to their purest essence. There is no room to be wordy, or to digress, or to swoon over the sound of your own words.

Within the hierarchy of the script, here are the elements you'll be dealing with: *dialogue, description* and *action* are joined together to make . . .

- **Scenes**. Some of those scenes are joined with other scenes to make a . . .
- **Sequence**. The scenes and sequences join together to make acts, which are punctuated by . . .
- **Plot points**, each of which sends the story into a spin, and leads to the next act.

THE SCENE

A scene is a compact unit of a script that takes place in one setting, usually within a short span of time. In theory, one good scene ought to lead to another; they are all connected by the imperative of the script as a whole. Each scene needs to create a reason for the next one to happen. One scene should flow organically into the next, and never with an ambling quality (deceptively ambling is okay), but instead with a true and authoritative sense of order. You are setting up the entire movie in the first act, and your task is to create scenes that help lay the foundation for all that follows.

If you write "INT. TRAIN STATION — DAY" and you show people waiting for a train there, and then suddenly we're on the train itself, the first scene has ended and the second one, "INT. TRAIN — DAY," has begun. If hours pass and the sky outside that train window is now dark, then you have yet another scene, "INT. TRAIN — NIGHT," even though it may involve the same characters in the same setting. Any break in place, action or time qualifies as the end of a scene.

Most scenes are short and to the point, running from a few lines of description and action and perhaps a line or two of dialogue (or even *no* dialogue, just action), to four or five pages long. A really, really important scene can go on even longer. (In the Copacabana scene in *GoodFellas*, Lorraine Bracco walks into the nightclub with her boyfriend, Ray Liotta, and through the way everyone treats him she realizes he's a big shot. His character is revealed through other people's eyes, and it takes this long, elaborate shot to do this well.) Quentin Tarantino likes to play with the notion of scene length (read the script of *Pulp Fiction*, and you'll find surprisingly protracted scenes). But right now, while you're beginning, try to keep your scenes to four pages or fewer. A genuinely crucial scene, if it's not too talky, might go slightly longer, perhaps five pages. But if you have an extremely long scene in your script, a movie executive probably isn't going to think you're being bold and interesting; he or she may think you don't understand the form.

Here's a scene that goes from page 10 to 11 in *Surrender, Dorothy*. Sara has just been killed, and her friends are reacting:

```
INT. LIVING ROOM — DAY

1. Pacing the room and SOBBING is ADAM LANGER,
   25, bookish, glasses, gay. On the couch are
   MADDY BENNETT, 25—not very pretty but intel-
   ligent and interesting—and her boyfriend,
   PETER COOPERMAN, also 25, athletic and lanky.
   They are all drinking hard liquor, and the
   room is littered with bottles and glasses.
   The whole place is a mess. There's a feeling
   of chaos in the air. Everyone is drunk,
   heading toward blotto oblivion.

                    MADDY
         You're not supposed to die at 25.
         It's unnatural.

                    ADAM
         You're supposed to die at 90.
         Sitting on your BarcaLounger,
         watching a rerun of Murder, She
         Wrote.

He sits down in a heap on the floor, putting
his head in his hands.
```

> ADAM (cont'd)
> Why wasn't she wearing her seat
> belt? The police said she would
> have survived.

2.
> PETER
> We should sue. We're all lawyers;
> we should get together and sue.

> MADDY
> Sue who? She ran a red light. And
> now she's dead.

She chokes on a SOB.

> ADAM
> We were going to get old together.
> We were going to live together
> someday. Two friends staying up
> late, talking. And now I'll never
> talk to her again.

He begins to SOB even harder. Peter clumsily
and self-consciously puts an arm around him.

3.
> MADDY
> It's okay, you can touch him, Pe-
> ter. It won't make you gay.

Peter regards her.

> PETER
> I'm fine with touching him, okay?

But he's clearly not, exactly. After a second, the two men uneasily move apart. Maddy
goes to the window, lighting a cigarette and

looking out, blowing the smoke through the screen.

4.
MADDY
The first day of Yale, there she was. She was so gorgeous. I never thought there was any chance we'd be friends.

PETER
So what changed it?

MADDY
I never told you this?

PETER
No.

5.
MADDY
That first night, we're lying there trying to go to sleep, and she tells me she knows how to sing backwards.

ADAM
I didn't know that.

MADDY
Yeah. And she launches into this backwards version of "Tears on My Pillow." It was so weird—I loved her right away.

ADAM
Oh, Sara. Jesus Christ. I can't believe this.

He tosses his glass against the wall, where
it SMASHES. No one comments or seems surprised. Maddy sits down in an armchair and
begins to sing "Tears on My Pillow"—backwards.

6.   MADDY
                   (singing)
      "Uoy t'nod rebmemer em/tub I reb-
      memer uoy/Ti t'nsaw gnol oga/Uoy
      ekorb ym traeh ni owt/Sraet no ym
      wollip/niap ni ym traeh, desuac
      yb uoy . . . Uoy, uoy uoy uoy . . ."

Then she bursts into tears and runs from the
room.

This is the first time that we've met Sara's friends (which
you can tell from the fact that their names are capitalized,
and that they are described in detail). I wanted to make sure
the reader has a strong sense of them and their predicament.
They're all in their mid-twenties, and their closest friend has
just been killed; they're shocked and freaked out, and I
needed to convey this immediately. Our first glimpse of the
friends is during a moment of emergency. I liked depicting
them that way; we don't need to witness the transformation
from mundane life to the impact of a death, the way we did
with Sara's mother, Natalie, who, within the space of the first
ten minutes of the movie (10 minutes = 10 pages) goes from
being an overinvolved mother and an ardent lover to a grieving mother. Showing a similar transformation among Sara's
friends would have slowed down the sense of propulsion,
which is so important in a screenplay.

    In fact, if you're having trouble with a scene and it doesn't seem to be going anywhere, it may be because the scene does not have any propulsive purpose in the script. Scenes are like participants in a relay race, passing a baton from one to the next until someone reaches the finish line. The "baton" here is the imperative, the reason behind the script, the set of ideas that you hope to convey. Any scene that does *not* serve this function—that does not pass the baton forward toward the finish line—has no place in your script. Remember what is supposed to happen in this act, and go back to your treatment to remind yourself, if necessary.

First in my scene come the descriptions (#1), both of the characters and their environment. Place and person are of equal importance here; they are both going to be visually depicted onscreen, and because of the mandate for irresistible watchability, I can't afford to let any of my characters be bland, or let the setting be neutral.

When the characters start to speak, we have to find out who they are from what they say (see the next chapter, "Six Characters in Search of a Screenwriter") and also gather information relevant to the story. Information in a screenplay—the hard facts that the audience must learn in order to follow the movie—should be spoon-fed in a way that is both subtle and appealing. As soon as the audience becomes aware that it is being asked to pay attention in a "learning" way, it loses interest.

This is quite different from other kinds of writing. People read books to learn new things, to enter into a world about which they had no previous knowledge. This is especially the case with nonfiction; a book that deals with a somewhat obscure topic (Dava Sobel's *Longitude*, Stephen Hawking's *A Brief History of Time*) can become immensely popular.

Readers crave facts that are found not only in science books but also in real-life stories that illustrate an entire subculture and introduce readers to a whole new vocabulary and set of experiences: *The Perfect Storm* (deep-sea fishing), *Into Thin Air* (climbing Mt. Everest). It happens in fiction, too. Many readers prefer novels that deal with a very particular subject, perhaps a historical one that provides plenty of hard facts about time and place and the social customs of the very specific world it illustrates: *The Alienist* (New York City crime at the turn of the century) *Mason & Dixon* (the eponymous land surveyors), even *Moby Dick* (whaling).

Movies, too, need to be "about" something, and they need to convey information. But anytime in a movie when a character makes a speech that overtly explains some basic and important fact, the audience members retreat into themselves. Their thoughts go elsewhere; they shift, they mentally fidget, they tune out the speech. At the end of *Psycho*, the detective played by Simon Oakland suddenly gives a long explanation of Anthony Perkins's character Norman Bates's emotional disturbance. The speech is totally out of place and it stops the film in its tracks. When the speech ends, the movie resumes once again, though briefly.

You sometimes find this phenomenon occurring toward the end of a movie; it's intended to clear up any confusion and pull together stray plot strands. There might be a leaden speech like this one:

BILL

You see, Morgan and Lesko had no idea we were onto them at the time, so they carried out their work in the processing plant as if no one was paying attention. But we saw that the beef they were approving really contained alarming levels of bacteria. Under federal guidelines, it was unsafe for consumption, and they knew it. But they had orders from the commissioner's office to approve it.

DON

But why? Why in hell would the commissioner do that?

BILL

Easy. Kickbacks. What's a few kids' lives in the short run, if you can be promised a long-term take of the graft?

Now, I've made up this ridiculous dialogue, but it is representative of a kind of pocket of dullness that sometimes hits a movie when "facts" need to be stated. In *Surrender, Dorothy*, Sara's friends are all lawyers, and I wanted to let the audience know this, although there was no interesting way to convey it visually. (I sometimes think there are so many architects in contemporary movies only because the filmmakers like to include the visual details of those cool slanting tables, and the blueprints and T-squares.)

The best way I found to show who Sara's friends are was to have Peter utter the line of dialogue at #2. This gives away a fact about their vocation, planted inside a larger point— that Peter wants to sue, wants to blame somebody for Sara's fatal car crash. The audience members can absorb the fact parenthetically, without having to be bored by it, because their minds will be focused on the *active* part of this fact: the potential lawsuit and the emotional response it conveys. A passive fact or bald explanation, however, as in my made-up dialogue between "Bill" and "Don," remains passive and cannot be absorbed with much interest. This is true of all elements in a script; those that are passive remain uninteresting and useless, like dead tissue; what's active is alive onscreen, and can regenerate itself and lead the audience right into the next scene.

Another fact in *Surrender, Dorothy* is offered just a few lines down (#3), when Maddy speaks to her boyfriend, Peter, and we learn from her quick comment that Adam is gay. I struggled with this one a little bit; originally, I had Adam saying that he had been "Sara's faggot friend," but that struck me as very false. In my experience, people don't refer to themselves that way, even in moments of crisis. And because we wouldn't be seeing Adam with a boyfriend, we couldn't learn that he was gay through *action* (an arm around another man, or a meaningful glance or a kiss), which is the obvious method of choice. As a character, he's not prone to conveying his sexuality through some *Boys in the Band* gesture or the way he dresses. Therefore, I needed to have someone else refer to the fact that Adam is gay, in a way that would convey other information, too. Otherwise it would all simply lie there as passive, dead-tissue fact. So when Maddy speaks her line, we really learn *three* new facts:

- that Adam is gay
- that there is awkwardness between Adam and Peter
- that there is tension between Maddy and Peter

These three facts provide important information that moves the script ahead into the next scene and beyond. We've learned details about the relationships between characters without having to wade through a long, talky scene, or read a long passage of flashback that shows the origins of these relationships. In fact, avoiding flashbacks was one of my primary challenges in writing this script. If Sara appeared to the characters in their memories, then the script would take on a quality that some people call haunting but I call maudlin.

The movie *To Gillian on Her 37th Birthday* dealt with a dead woman (Michelle Pfeiffer) who lived on in the minds of the people who grieved for her. The device seemed awkward to me; unless you take such a device all the way and make a dead person actually *show up* (*Truly, Madly, Deeply*; *Ghost*), then you're left in a kind of impressionistic limbo of memory and sentimentality. I wanted to avoid that trap completely, so I made sure that Sara didn't appear at all. What we would learn about her—and what we would learn about her friends' relationships with her—would have to be offered in another way.

I felt that I could get away with the other characters discussing Sara in a very direct way because she was recently dead—and people do talk about the recently dead. Here, Maddy overtly describes Sara to the audience (#4), but it seems acceptable to me in a eulogistic, reflective way, especially if one of the details we learn about Sara is idiosyncratic and unusual (#5), and we see that detail in action. (#6)

Successful scenes in movies are filled with action and motion, both literally and figuratively. Even if a scene involves a confrontation between two characters in as unpromising a place as an elevator—an enclosed, interior space with very

little besides a NO SMOKING sign that qualifies as decor—
something else must happen in the scene to give it life and
pass the baton to the next scene. Maybe another character
gets on the elevator, and changes the extent to which the two
characters can speak freely, thus revealing the secretiveness
of what they're saying. Maybe the elevator stalls. Maybe
someone has a fear of small spaces. Maybe the "fact" we
learn is simply that one character is incredibly impatient, revealed by the way he keeps repeatedly punching an already
lit button, and perhaps this impatience will play a key role
later in the movie.

You have to make these sorts of choices as you write your
scenes, and they'll be based not just on the idea that "something has to happen" within a scene, but rather on the idea
that something *relevant* has to happen, something that keeps
propelling the script forward. The viewer must want to know
more. The writer has to ensure that the viewer possesses this
need, and that it is satisfied.

This is very different from the way you might approach a
scene in a piece of fiction or journalism. In a screenplay, your
approach is both more literal and more subtle. It's more literal because you don't have long paragraphs of memory to
rely upon. This isn't Proust.* If someone is forgetful, you
must *show* her in the act of forgetting. If someone is a great
cook, we must *see* the incredible meal he has made, and long

---

*Actually, Harold Pinter wrote a terrific, unproduced script published
under the title *The Proust Screenplay*. It's worth reading, in that it's a
distillation of *Remembrance of Things Past*, an impressionistic take on
Proust's ideas about memory, childhood and French society. The version of Proust that did make it to the screen—*Swann in Love*, written
by someone other than Pinter and starring Jeremy Irons and Ornella
Mutti, neither of whom is French—was less impressionistic but inevitably more melodramatic and stilted.

to eat it (*Like Water for Chocolate, Big Night*). Sight is the guiding sense during a movie, and a screenplay needs to rely on an exaggerated version of the maxim "Show, don't tell." This maxim is also one of the rules of fiction writing, which you likely heard in the first workshop you ever took. Of course, with fiction, you can "show" in plenty of different ways. We might suddenly be hurtled all the way back to 1897, where we stay for pages and pages, and the reader doesn't mind at all. But in your screenplay, all the important details you show about characters and place and situation need to be acted out or outlined in the presence of the audience.

If you have a character who is a kleptomaniac, for example, and you *don't* show him stealing something, then you are missing an opportunity to illustrate the held-breath tension inherent in the act of stealing, as well as the excitement connected with the illicit act, not to mention the essential peek at the kleptomaniac's nature, and, of course, the suspense of whether or not he will be caught. It's related to that adage about the theater: "If there's a telephone onstage, it has to ring." In a movie, you must be sure to put a metaphorical telephone onscreen so that it has a *chance* to ring.

Because a scene is a series of moments taking place in one particular location, as soon as the setting changes, the scene is over. But there are other qualities that determine when the scene should end. When beginning a scene, you have to ask yourself (and refer to your treatment if necessary): "What do I hope to accomplish here?" And when you think the scene is finished, ask yourself: "Have I accomplished it?" If you haven't, then the scene needs to be reworked—although not interminably. If you get really stuck, move on; you want to keep going forward and build scenes that create acts, and acts that create a screenplay. If you reach your goal within the scene, make sure that the scene also contributes to the forward motion of the movie, leading the character through the necessary changes, and the story toward the necessary plot point.

What makes a good scene? First of all, an interesting setting contributes a great deal. One of the most common mistakes made by writers attempting a first screenplay is constantly to put their characters in restaurants or cafes or bars. "What's wrong with that?" a writer might ask. "My friends and I spend a lot of time in restaurants and cafes and bars." What's wrong is that generally such places aren't visually dynamic, because they literally force the characters into a sitting position—into a kind of *stasis*—and the emphasis is usually on the talking. Which means that we're more attuned to the aural and less to the visual, so the visual sense is not being stimulated adequately.

An odd exception is *My Dinner with André*, which takes place entirely in a restaurant over dinner. But this movie works because its central "device"—its setting and the fact that it occurs in what's known as "real time" (the passage of time isn't compressed or "suggested," so two hours in the restaurant = two hours onscreen)—makes it special. I really enjoyed it, but as a friend of mine commented, she couldn't wait for the waiter to show up at the table or the busboy to pour more water. It was the only "action" in the entire movie.

Find alternatives to restaurants and cafes and bars. *Get your characters outside.* Otherwise, the movie will suffer the fate of Woody Allen's aptly named *Interiors*—self-conscious claustrophobia. Exteriors open up a movie, give it a little fresh air, and make the audience itself feel refreshed. Make a list of ten good exterior locations for your characters. Then make another list of ten good interior locations. The second list is a little trickier; while it's fairly easy to come up with exteriors such as "duck pond" or "tennis court," it may be slightly tougher to think of indoor places where you can put your characters without creating that sensation of claustrophobia. But there are such places—interiors that hold more possibilities than a restaurant—such as the theater, the department store, the classroom, the bowling alley, someone's unusual home, a barn, an attic, a dusty basement, a Mafia-based "social club," an automobile showroom, a health club, to name just a few. It all depends on the scene's dramatic significance.

The best scenes in screenplays contain small pleasures and surprises: an unexpected gesture, an offbeat moment, a shocking exchange of dialogue. While I realize the visuals are being stressed in this chapter (in part because experienced writers often have a very weak idea about what is visual), what gets said and sung and sounded is also extremely important in terms of furnishing a solid scene.

Just as no scene should be overly long, no character's dialogue in a scene should go on for too long. Think about what happens when someone dominates conversation at a dinner party. If the monologue is really fascinating, then everyone will listen raptly. But if it's *not* fascinating, then everyone will be aware of how much this person is dominating, and will leave before dessert.

A scene is a moment in time that signifies something, captured and bracketed within a larger structure. The scene carries out a smaller version of the mission of the larger structure; it's an emissary, delivering the meaning or message of the movie, although that message may be buried or disguised. If you know the "message," and you know how to thread it through the entire script (this is sometimes referred to as the "through-line"), then your script will be on track.

THE SEQUENCE

Some writers feel constrained by the requisite brevity of the typical movie scene. Perhaps you're used to writing books, and to making them as long as they need to be. Or perhaps you've written for a newspaper and are used to space limitations—but even so, you've never felt as constrained as you do right now. (It's strange how much needs to be conveyed in so few pages, and yet filling 120 pages can often be torture.) It might make more sense, psychologically, to think of your script in terms of scenes and sequences rather than just scenes. A full sequence gives you the time you need to make your point; there's no page limit.

All scripts contain sequences—a series of thematically connected scenes that are powerful and memorable and direct the reader right through the story (the wedding sequence in *The Godfather*, the chase sequence in *The French Connection*). Think of some of the movies you've enjoyed, and try to locate their significant sequences. I'm reminded of the sequence at the beginning of *Four Weddings and a Funeral*, in which Hugh Grant's character and his friend are rushing off to a wedding. The sequence, with all its comic timing and good lines, introduces us to the protagonist as well as some of the other characters, and establishes part of the premise of the movie—as promised by the title.

And then there's the sequence at the opening of Alfred Hitchcock's *Shadow of a Doubt*. Joseph Cotten's character, Charlie, a.k.a. "the Merry Widow Murderer," is wanted by the police. When they show up at his boardinghouse, he makes his escape. During a train ride, heading to the all-American home of his sister and her family, he affects a limp and pretends to be in obviously poor medical shape. When Charlie gets off the train and walks along the platform toward his waiting relatives, his limp slowly disappears and his pace increases, so that by the time he's being welcomed by his sister and her family, he's transformed into a new person: gone is the murderer eluding the law; gone is the fake limp. In their place is the confident, easygoing, beloved Uncle Charlie.

This swift and exciting sequence at the opening of the movie shows us the development of both a character (a dangerous *poseur*) and a setup. The new persona is complete, and his hideout is waiting. The author of this marvelous screenplay is playwright Thornton Wilder, who was very perceptive about the complexity and darkness within small-town America.

Let's try to establish a sequence for *Bay Parkway*, starting with the first scene that features the girl riding on the subway train. Suppose, after that scene ends and the opening credits roll, we stay with the girl and watch her get off the train and squeeze her way between commuters. Perhaps we see her go up the stairs of the subway station and into the bright sun of the Brooklyn day, all the while singing to herself a popular Andrews Sisters' song. We watch her sing as she hurries, and we see her interact with different vendors and neighbors and friends. As she walks through the neighborhood, we get a guided tour of her world—the world of the movie. We meet most of the central characters, too: the baker's wife, from whom the girl buys a loaf of seeded rye to give her mother. The man at the shoe-repair shop, where she picks up her shoes and listens to two customers discussing the war in somber voices.

She enters her building and runs up the five flights to her apartment, not even out of breath. As she bursts into the apartment, the bread still warm, singing the song, full of a kind of deluded youthful optimism, she is met by several sets of staring eyes. Her mother is there, and her father, and a few neighbors. Everyone has been crying. All the adults look up at her. She stops singing. In a tiny voice, she says to her mother, "I brought you some bread." Her father tells her that the neighbor's son Michael has been killed. The bread falls to the floor. The sequence ends.

From this sequence we get a sense of the character's whole world and the central drama at the heart of her world—namely the war—which, until the moment of her neighbor's son's death, has merely been an abstract concept, announced in newspapers, but which is suddenly brought home to Bay Parkway. The sequence builds character, place and drama, all at once.

SUBPLOTS

A subplot weaves through all three acts of a screenplay, creating necessary complications. There may even be more than one subplot. A script that doesn't have enough complications will feel flat and empty. The subplot also serves to set the main plot in relief. My friend Mark Saltzman insists that the subplot isn't an actual separate story at all but merely an extension of the main story. Because all subplots involving secondary characters are inextricably linked to the main plot that concerns the main characters, he feels these subplots shouldn't be thought of as separate. Although I don't entirely agree, I understand his point and want to emphasize that a secondary plot does need to have some significant relationship to the primary plot, or else it shouldn't be included. Don't go out of your way to pull a subplot out of thin air; it should arise fairly naturally from what's already there. Don't force a story line to come; instead, try to take your characters deeper, following them farther than you might have thought to, learning interesting details about them that might lend themselves well to being amplified into a related mini-story, or subplot. In *We Have to Stop*, the so-called subplot involves the relationship between Dr. Joslin's widow, Miriam, and Carrie's father—a relationship that's an outgrowth of the main plot: the relationship between Carrie and Tim.

Your subplot should be introduced in the first act, given its own complexities in act two, and resolved in act three. The subplot in *Good Will Hunting* involved the professor's long-standing ambivalent relationship with the therapist, played by Robin Williams; another subplot concerned the therapist's struggle with grief over the loss of his wife. Both of these asides were woven gracefully into the fabric of the movie, and as a result, *Good Will Hunting* felt packed with characters and ideas and motion.

PLOT POINTS

As your scenes and sequences accrue and the primary and secondary premises of the script are laid out, you'll head toward the plot point at the end of the act that will send the movie into a new direction. It's important that you know what your plot points are going to be—and have them worked out in your treatment—before you start writing the script. (Sometimes you may have more than two in your script; the second act of a movie with many twists and turns might include an extra plot point that spins the story off into a new direction but doesn't actually end the act.)

In the screenplay of *Surrender, Dorothy*, here's the basic story (I'm referring to the screenplay version; the novel version is an entirely different entity, as I'll discuss later): A group of friends in their twenties, who have been sharing a house in the Hamptons every summer since college, go out to the house for the season, and on the way there, one of them, a woman named Sara (whose voice we heard talking to her mother on the answering machine) is killed in a car accident. Her friends—including her college roommate, Maddy, and Maddy's fiancé, Peter (who were going to get married this summer)—are hysterical, and so is her mother, Natalie. (Peter had once been involved with Sara, before Maddy.) Maddy calls the wedding off. At the funeral, Sara's friends casually tell Natalie that she's welcome to visit them at the house anytime. And at the end of the act, she does. She drives out to the house and moves in. *This* is the first real plot point. (Sara's death occurs right at the beginning of the movie and is inextricable from the setup; it can't really be said to send the movie in a whole new direction because the movie hasn't gone in any particular direction yet.)

In act two, Natalie convinces Maddy not to cancel the wedding; she explains that she had always wanted to make a wedding for Sara, and now she won't get a chance to do so. Natalie asks if she can throw Maddy and Peter's wedding. Maddy feels sorry for her, and agrees. But as the days and weeks pass, Natalie gets overinvolved in every detail of the wedding—insisting on doing things *her* way.

Meanwhile, an attraction builds between Natalie and Peter, who is reminded of Sara by the resemblance of mother and daughter. One night, at a rave in Montauk, very high on a hallucinogen that's being passed around, Peter kisses Natalie. And Maddy sees it happen. The wedding is off again, Maddy announces in anger, and this serves as the second plot point, sending the story into yet another direction.

Now, at the beginning of act three, disorder abounds. No one is speaking to anyone. Everyone decides to leave the house for good. Natalie and Peter separately beg Maddy's forgiveness, but Maddy won't budge. The wedding guests, who haven't been told the wedding is off again, start to arrive at the house. These guests include Maddy's mother, Mrs. Bennett, who has been very cold to Maddy since her engagement to Peter, who is Jewish. Maddy has a showdown with her mother and realizes that Mrs. Bennett hasn't behaved like much of a mother, but that Natalie—despite her annoying overinvolvement, and perhaps *because* of it—has. Maddy forgives Natalie and announces that the wedding is *on* yet again. Natalie will be Maddy's maid of honor, as Sara was going to be. At the wedding, which Maddy and Peter had feared was going to be only a tribute to Sara, Natalie is totally appropriate. To everyone's surprise she leaves Sara out of her toast to the couple and makes the wedding a real celebration of Peter and Maddy's love.

The script follows the traditional three-act structure very closely, although it's no accident that it does. The novel, which as I said is completely different, didn't really work as a screenplay, and had to be rethought. I made sure to insert plot points that would anchor the script and reroute it at crucial junctures.

Plot points don't exist in space, floating freely. As you continue writing over the weeks, heading toward the plot point at the end of your first act, you'll see that every scene and sequence you write must be with an eye toward the movement at the end of the act, the sudden change. The plot points need to arise out of a carefully laid set of circumstances. The circumstances of the screenplay version of *Surrender, Dorothy* are fairly clear: a young woman dies, her mother moves in, she drives everyone nuts, there's a sexual encounter, the wedding is off. Then one of the characters, Maddy, discovers the meaning of having a mother, and forgives Natalie. The wedding is on again. Finally we see the wedding, with all its festivity and emotion.

I'm partial to ceremonies, both in life and in art. A ceremony scene onscreen can be an occasion for high humor (*Four Weddings and a Funeral*) or something more muted and contemplative (*Hannah and Her Sisters*, which is centered on holiday dinners). In a ceremony scene, you can actually let a character give a toast or eulogy or some other kind of speech, talking movingly or humorously in one long monologue in a way you might be wary of anywhere else in the film.

The scenes in the first act of your movie will gather volume and content as they move along. Each one should lead to the next, in a natural fashion. Finally, when all has been said and done to set up the story and you're on page 20-something or approaching page 30, you must drop in your first plot point.

Suppose you're writing a movie in which a couple is happily married and preparing for the birth of their first child, and we see them together at the beginning, and there's a sequence in which we follow them to a horrible, fluorescent-lit baby emporium, where they look at various items, and the wife comments mildly that it's bad luck to actually bring any of these items into the house until the baby is born. Then they go to his brother's house for lunch, and we see a funny, chummy relationship between the wife and her brother-in-law, who is single. The couple goes home, makes love, and the husband sings a little song to their future baby, resting his head on his wife's stomach.

The next day the wife goes to work, where her friends surprise her with an office baby shower. We've now met family and friends—all the important figures in the film. At the end of the party, though, the wife isn't feeling well, so she goes into her office to sit down, and then she begins to hemorrhage. This is the first plot point—it not only changes the actual plot of the movie; it changes the *tone* of the movie as well. We have gone from a dreamy, giddy, *Barefoot in the Park*-with-an-impending-child scenario to medical fear and uncertainty.

Some version of this transformation ought to take place in your script. The plot point needs to alter everything. We might not understand all its ramifications right away, and in fact the tone does not have to shift as dramatically as it does in this pregnancy movie, but it needs to affect the characters and their actions in a significant way. It's sort of like a chemical reaction; the plot point is a new element added to a mixture, which then totally changes the chemistry of that mixture. The reader of your screenplay is left with all kinds of questions: What's going to happen next? How will the characters get out of this situation? How will it all be resolved? In a sense, a plot point in the first act takes the reader from security to insecurity—or, sometimes, from insecurity to security. But it always involves a major change, and after it takes place, then nothing will be the same for the rest of the movie.

STAYING WITH YOUR SCRIPT

By the time you begin the second act, you will know how it's all done; you'll understand the way scenes and sequences combine to create an act, and the way a plot point changes the direction of that act. Act two picks up where act one left off. It's true that act two is usually twice as long, but so much of what you'll need to include has already been set out for you; you know the central premise of the story. Act two is the place where that story gets elaborated and built upon, layered, and truly *told*. The main character starts to undergo profound change, the subplot is continued and the action moves forward toward the next big plot point that ends the act.

While all screenwriters nod their heads in empathy when another writer speaks of having "second act problems," my sense is that these problems may not arise as often for writers who are used to other forms. The second act is often richer, slower, more textured and intricate than the first. It requires the writer to possess thoughtfulness and the ability to see a piece of writing as if from above, as if looking down at the entire project. The second act is tough but rewarding; it allows you to explore the characters and the premise of the script more fully. It allows you to really *write*. Hold fast to your script through the second act; work on any problems that may arise, refer constantly to your treatment or your index cards, or both. Don't give up at this point; you're in the heart of the script now, and unless a problem really paralyzes you, try to move ahead through the complexities and right into the disorder that often ends the act.

Act three is a time of resolution; this act should be "cleaner" than the kind of writing you usually do. It involves the sometimes hasty task of making everything okay (or making it not okay, but doing so definitively). It's a swift act that sets everything right and leaves an impression, a resonance. All endings should be knockouts (such as in *The Godfather*, with the calm scene of Al Pacino at the baby's christening intercut with the scenes of the systematic rubout of the other characters, or the long walk down the road at the close of *The Third Man*).

Ideally, there will be a satisfying symmetry in your screenplay that is revealed through a look at the beginning and ending. (In *Grand Hotel*, for instance, a clerk at the beginning grouses that nothing happens at Grand Hotel—and then at the end, after all the separate drama-packed stories of life at the hotel have been told, we see him again, still complaining that nothing ever happens around there. And in *The Crowd*, a silent movie directed by King Vidor, we zoom in on a crowd of people and learn one couple's specific stories. At the end of the movie, we pull back from these characters, seeing them once again as the anonymous faces of the crowd.)

The ending of your screenplay may amplify or contradict or merely reflect upon the opening. However you decide to end your script, remember that nothing is set in stone. This is only a first draft, and any muddled thinking or misguided direction on your part—and chances are there will be some—can be remedied later on, when you start the crucial process of revision.

Chapter Six

Six Characters in Search of a Screenwriter

Most books about screenwriting dwell at length on the issue of character, as well they should. A poorly developed character can sink a film, making it feel false and dissatisfying, while a complex and convincing character can become the centerpiece of the entire enterprise. But a good deal of the space in many screenwriting books devoted to character includes the information you most likely learned in your first creative writing workshop: the notion that characters need to be "rounded," with a past and a present and a future, and that their lives should be adorned with details. This is all useful advice for the beginning writer, but I'm working under the assumption that you already know the basics of developing a character. What you may know less about, however, is how to develop a character expressly for a screenplay.

Movie characters are different from characters in fiction. For one thing, they tend to be *bigger* (Jake La Motta in *Raging Bull*, Christy Brown in *My Left Foot*). They do and say more unusual things, they engage in outsized activities, and they interact with other characters in ways that are distinctly cinematic. The world of film people tends to feel not like the real world as we know it but, instead, like some alternative screen-world that we accept whenever we go to the movies—so much so that we convince ourselves it *is* real. And it is, in a way; it's the "real" world according to Hollywood, in which Aristotle's notions of art imitating life don't apply. In movies, art *exaggerates* life. Life becomes bigger, bolder, more brilliantly hued, as well as funnier, more tragic, more action-packed, more filled with coincidence, not to mention sexier, and definitely more sentimental. We understand that we will have to suspend our disbelief whenever we walk into the theater, and we do so without hesitation.

The biggest distinction between prose characters and those created specifically for movies is that the ones in movies are known to us not primarily by what they feel or think or fantasize about, but by what they *do* (also, to a somewhat lesser extent, by what they *say*). If, as a writer, you've been raised on a steady diet of Henry James, you're probably going to have some trouble adjusting when you start writing screenplays. In the kinds of novels you're used to, the interior life of the characters is as essential as the world that surrounds them—specifically the social customs and conventions of the day. Characters whose complex inner lives are the key to revelations will need some reimagining for the screen.

Which isn't to say that screen characters have to be lovably simpleminded, like Forrest Gump, or foulmouthed misanthropes, like Jack Nicholson's Melvin in *As Good as It Gets*. But all characters do need to share certain qualities, specifically:

- a clarity to their personalities, spelled out simply and easily for audiences
- memorable idiosyncrasies or personality specifics
- a distinctive and clearly stated imperative

You may chafe at the idea that a character "needs" to be of a certain type in a screenplay. Certainly there is no equivalent restriction in most other forms of writing. But a very complex character in a novel may not necessarily appear complex onscreen, where there isn't the opportunity to plumb the psychic depths or the host of experiences that caused him to turn out a certain way. A character who only *suggests* complexity may appear muted and therefore frustrating, forcing the audience to make inferences that aren't necessarily true. It's much better to demonstrate complexity through action and interaction.

It's also important to remember that when you're writing a part for a character, you're really writing a part for an actor. Actors want to use their talents fully; they choose roles that are memorable, with characters who can be quoted ("I'm mad as hell and I'm not going to take it anymore!" "La dee dah . . .") or imitated or simply remembered with awe (*Sling Blade*, *Forrest Gump*, *Elephant Man*, *Misery*). You should always be aware of casting when you write a screenplay, at least in some recess of your mind. This may seem impure, on some level; it's definitely different from the advice I give my fiction students, which is: "Don't worry about your readers. Don't even think about them, who they are, what they like, how you can satisfy them. Don't think about writing directly 'to' anyone. The work will only come out forced."

But when you're writing a script, you might do well to imagine that a part is being written for a particular actor, someone you admire and who you think would be right for the role. In your descriptions of the character, don't get overly specific, because if an actor can't imagine inhabiting the part, he or she won't choose to be in the movie. Define your characters through their "type," banning clichés from the description. It's a real challenge to find the right adjectives and other kinds of words that will breathe life into characters and make them attractive and challenging to actors. An uncastable screenplay equals an unproducible screenplay; you aren't writing in a vacuum, and your script has to appeal to the people who ought to be in it.

Because most studio-produced movies have characters who are spelled out very clearly through the things they *do,* as opposed to the things they think or feel, the actor may have to do plenty of work to get a sense of the cadences and nuances and history of the character. But the audience should not have to resort to emotional sleuthing in order to understand the character.

Onscreen, a sort of personality "shorthand" usually takes place. Who someone is may be determined more by what he eats for dinner, and how, and with whom, than by what he feels or thinks about when he's eating that dinner. The conduit to those thoughts and feelings is the *action.* In a movie, the action is never allowed to stop. Continual movement is essential to the flow of the story.

THE ARC OF A CHARACTER

Continual movement is essential to your characters, too. The arc of a character refers to the changes a character undergoes over the course of three acts. It's a phrase I don't care for, but it's used so often that you need to know it. If you understand screenplay structure, you'll understand the arc, because it travels through the acts in a similar fashion. In the beginning the character is established, only to be confronted by something (or to set up a confrontation by him- or herself) by the end of the act. Now, the changes in situation lead to relevant character changes—subtle or not-so-subtle shifts in mood, behavior, beliefs or actions. All of which lead toward further changes and disorder by the end of the second act. In the third act, resolution takes place and order is restored. We finally get to see the character for who he or she is at the end of the movie: restored to an original state, maybe, or altered in some significant way.

If the arc isn't there—if the changes can't be seen by the naked eye—then the movie won't work. Do people really change like this in life? Rarely. But movies aren't life, nor are they literature, so they shouldn't be held to novelistic standards, either. While tracking a character's arc may imply a simplicity of understanding that seems reductive, the form demands it.

CHARACTER ANALYSIS

Writers who started out working in forms other than screenplays often have a particularly hard time making the shift to "screen" characters. Because you already have a subtle understanding about characterization, you may feel you've got an advantage over everyone else. This is untrue. In the long run, your characters may wind up more interesting, but you will have to translate your abilities into screen language in order to let your characters shine. To that end, I've developed a detailed character analysis questionnaire that you might want to fill out in order not only to nail down the history of your character, but also to dig up the specific qualities that might be brought out by that history. You may tend to be skeptical of such questionnaires, likening them to dumb quizzes in women's magazines ("What's Your Bisexual IQ?" or "Does He Really Love You, or Is He Just Using You?"), but this one is helpful.

Character Analysis Questionnaire

1. If you met this character at a dinner party and sat next to him or her all evening, what's the strongest impression you would take away from the experience?
2. How are his or her table manners? Describe anything unusual.
3. Has he or she ever experienced the death of someone close? Describe that experience and its effects.
4. What's the sexual fantasy to which he or she always returns?
5. If relevant, is he or she sexually active? And what is he/she like in bed?
6. Describe a dream that the character had, and then do a brief dream interpretation.
7. What were/are his or her parents like? Which one was he or she closer to?
8. What was the most traumatic experience this character has ever had? Go into detail.
9. What was his or her most pleasurable moment?
10. Favorite book?
11. Favorite movie?
12. If he or she were to commit a crime, what would it be?

13. Greatest weakness? Be specific, and give an example of this weakness in action.

14. Greatest strength? Again, be specific and give an example of this strength in action.

15. Does he or she like animals? Which ones, and why?

16. Which of the seven deadly sins applies to this character?

17. Pretend that you're a therapist and your character has just walked into your office for the first time. You say to the character, "Tell me why you're here." What does the character say, and how does he or she behave while saying it? Write down the therapy monologue of the character word for word.

18. Does he or she have a nervous habit? What is it?

19. What part of his or her body is the character vainest about? Most self-conscious about?

20. What is your character's biggest secret, and why? Also, who knows about this secret, if anyone?

CHEMISTRY

Screenplays aren't simply elaborate showcases for disparate characters, and even those so-called character-driven movies need to be fueled by the twin engines of plot and imperative. No character should ever be thought of as separate from his or her context; every character occupies a screen society that involves other, complementary characters. Well-drawn characters in action will have a certain chemistry between them (Katharine Hepburn and Spencer Tracy in *Adam's Rib*, Morgan Freeman and Jessica Tandy in *Driving Miss Daisy*, Geena Davis and Susan Sarandon in *Thelma and Louise*). Sometimes this chemistry verges on a combustibility that needs to be managed and exploited by the writer.

Suppose you're trying to write a romantic comedy and you want to find two characters, male and female, who will end up together by the end of the movie, thus satisfying the traditional formula for romantic comedies. Studio executives claim that they're always looking for the next big romantic comedy, but in fact very few of these screenplays get produced. Some of this has to do with the potential for romantic comedies to be "low concept," as well as the fact that it's really hard to write a very funny movie. And if the chemistry between actors/characters isn't there, no one will want to see them arguing or being best friends or falling into bed together. Chemistry isn't just about sex, or a nostalgic history shared by two characters; it's also about that X-factor, the unknown quality that gives certain movies a boost, and makes others fail.

You can heighten or even create a chemical excitement between your characters—whether it's sexual, emotional, intellectual or otherwise. Think about the character questionnaire you just filled out; now fill it out again, but this time answer as many of the questions as possible about your character (character A) from the point of view of character B. You'll learn something about the way character B sees character A, and also about the way he or she sees the world. Then reverse it, answering the questions about character B, both from *your* point of view and from the point of view of character A. What you want to locate in this haystack is friction, excitement, differences between characters that could lead to interesting conflicts onscreen. Movies travel from conflict to resolution (and sometimes back again, more than once), and this path can be seen in miniature within the characters' personalities and interactions.

Let's look at a movie everyone knows: *The Wizard of Oz*. After the cyclone, when Dorothy finds herself in a strange land among strange creatures, all she wants to do is find her way home. Home becomes the central, defining imperative of both the movie and of Dorothy herself. The other characters she meets *react* and *respond* to Dorothy's imperative. The Scarecrow, Tin Man and Lion all want to help her achieve her goal, and there is a mutuality at work, because they have goals too (exemplified through their characters), all of which can supposedly be achieved through the Wizard. The Wicked Witch, on the other hand, reacts and responds *counter* to Dorothy's imperative. The personality tics and traits of all the characters work beautifully together in the film, with each character given his or her moment to show off those special qualities.

When I think of ensemble performing, I'm reminded of Prokofiev's *Peter and the Wolf*, in which each instrument represents an animal and has a musical phrase that repeats throughout the score. It's very similar in screenplays. Each character has a particular personality, laid out with clarity, along with one or two tics or shticks that we learn about and can even come to anticipate.

In the exciting finale of an early Alfred Hitchcock movie, *Young and Innocent*, a literal tic is the giveaway. The murderer on the loose has a facial twitch; everyone is looking for him, but he hides out onstage, playing in a swing band, all of whose musicians are in blackface. We see a close-up of the drummer's twitching face, and as the tension builds he begins playing out of rhythm. It's a thrilling scene, in which Hitchcock reveals the murderer to the audience before the characters see him, letting us in on the secret, a particular shtick of Hitchcock's.

Characters have imperatives, too, which may be in concordance with one another, or may be in conflict. Even if you're not specifically writing an ensemble piece such as *Swingers*, *Singles* or *The Big Chill*, be aware of the ways in which your characters affect one another—and the entire script—based on who they are and what we know about them.

CLARITY

A character who is presented with clarity is someone whom you will remember. For many years, my oldest friend, Martha, and I have had a slightly tongue-in-cheek theory that there are two types of people whom one tends to meet socially. We call them "moose heads" and "bookshelves." Those we put in the first category are the sort of people with very big personalities, who assert their presence all the time, figuratively thrusting their heads forward into any room they're in, like a stuffed moose head on a wall. The people we call bookshelves, on the other hand, are those who *don't* have a big presence in a room. Instead, they seem to stay flush with the wall the way shelves do, quietly fitting in.

Characters in books or stories can be either moose heads or bookshelves. But characters in movies are almost always moose heads. This doesn't mean that all movie characters are extroverts; some are unbearably shy or antisocial or about as much of a chatterbox as Holly Hunter in *The Piano*. But they are all full of clearly defined personality, and therefore they assert themselves forcefully into a movie. A quietly struggling and appealing character like Helen Hunt's Carol in *As Good as It Gets* is a moose head masquerading as a bookshelf, but she's obviously really a moose head. Bookshelves don't have hidden glamour or give memorable speeches in a film or win Academy Awards; moose heads do. Carol has a determination about her that is palpable; we see it not in relation to nothing, but mostly in relation to other people: Jack Nicholson's character, Greg Kinnear's character and the character of her son, who is asthmatic and whom she loves with a fierceness that illuminates her performance. Taking care of her son involves real work that drains her emotionally, physically and financially. We learn about how worn down Carol is through her interactions with her little boy, and through her constant motion.

The situation is made more poignant by the presence of her mother (Shirley Knight), whose dreams and hopes for her daughter are clear. They are, in fact, Carol's own dreams and hopes for herself, but she can't come out and say them onscreen in any way that won't feel stilted, so we need someone else who can. (Note: no matter what shameless tricks you may perform in a screenplay, *never, never have a character talk to him- or herself in a mirror.* A character who needs a mirror to reveal things to the audience really needs another character onscreen to serve as that mirror.)

Clarity occurs when a character is shown very specifically and pointedly to be a certain way and do things in a certain way, because of a *central need*. If we don't know the character's central need, then we don't really know enough about the character.

Think about one of your close friends. What is his or her dominating need? This may be a difficult question to answer, one that requires carefully examining your friend's life and loves and goals. One woman, for instance, may have a need for financial success that overrides everything else; another may have a need to fail, however unconscious that need. A female friend may have an intense need to become pregnant, and her window of fertility is closing soon. A man may need to be seen in public with beautiful women in order to prove his worth. Another may need to stop being haunted by memories of a tortured childhood.

Be as specific as you can when creating a central need for your character; start with a larger, psychological sense of need and move ahead from there, finding the particular way this need will manifest itself *visually* and in *action,* over the course of a movie. Think of five specific, scenic examples of ways you can demonstrate that need onscreen. But need is just the start; all movies deal with both need and an obstacle to that need. Otherwise, there's no conflict, and without conflict, your project is doomed.

Let's say the friend who wants to get pregnant so badly finally does. And just as she's about to tell everyone the news, she learns that her husband is having an affair, and that therefore her marriage is in jeopardy. What should she do? Have the child she's always wanted, pretending that she doesn't know about the affair? Have the child and kick her husband out? Have an abortion and break up her marriage? The supposedly simple need to have a child is suddenly challenged by obstacles, and, because of this, the need shifts subtly.

Now the woman learns that it's one thing to long for a child in an abstract way, but quite another actually to have one and be forced to confront all the complexities that motherhood entails. If this were a screenplay, the acts would break like this:

Act one: Wanting a child. At the end of the act comes the plot point of getting pregnant.

Act two: Being pregnant, and being deliriously happy. Soon, however, the happiness is intruded upon by the realization that the husband is unfaithful, which is another plot point. Now the woman goes into action (and consequently her character becomes fuller and more interesting), hiring a detective to find out who the husband's lover is, all the while experiencing morning sickness and other indignities of pregnancy. Finally she makes an appointment to have an abortion, a decision that provides the second plot point and ends the act.

In act three, the woman goes for the abortion with great misgivings, and her husband follows her there and confronts her in the waiting room, begging her not to go through with it. The affair is over, he says. He wants them to have the baby. She agrees not to have the abortion; she really still does want the baby. Her husband is thrilled, and he embraces her and says it will all be fine, he'll change, they'll go into couples' therapy, they'll become closer than ever, et cetera. She looks at him and says no, I'm going to have the baby, but our marriage is over.

This is probably a rotten idea for a movie, but it does illustrate how a character's simple, defining need at the start is confronted with an obstacle, which shifts the need and changes the direction of the movie. Through the interplay of need and obstacle, a whole story unfolds, and the character unfolds too, becoming less monomaniacal and more complex. In this way, *story informs character, and character informs story*. They are inextricable from each other in a way that you may be unused to.

Examine the main character of your screenplay and ascertain his or her central need. Then be more specific about that need; tailor it to fit the story, and tailor the story to fit the need. It's a give-and-take process, in which you slowly discover the subtle alterations you must make in both character and story. When character and story are working well, the two should dovetail beautifully, creating a true sense of clarity.

IDIOSYNCRASIES AND DEFINING TRAITS

There are small oddities and larger personality attributes that fill out the characters in a script, making them distinctly themselves and unlike anyone else. As soon as one of these characteristics is established, it shouldn't be dropped from the script, but instead needs to be used again for full effect. If, for instance, you establish early on that your character is afraid of dogs, and you see this fear in action in a scene that *defines* the fear, then by the time the character falls in love with a woman (and subsequently learns that the woman is the devoted owner of a Doberman pinscher named Schatzi), the audience responds in anticipation of the character's reaction upon learning that there's a big scary dog behind the bedroom door of his true love. The idiosyncrasy is set up, and then followed up on later.

Such idiosyncrasies should never be put into a script just for their humor value or to make the script seem quirky. They need some larger function, too. In this case, the dog phobia gives us a sense of the character's foibles, making him human and, at least in movie terms, "complex." Movie complexity is different from fiction or essay or play complexity; it is less *internally* complex. (Actually, it is probably less complex overall.)

A novel, as opposed to a script, gives the writer an entire volume to establish exactly who a character really is. In *Madame Bovary*, for instance, we have Emma Bovary, an extremely complicated narcissist whose actions inevitably lead to destruction. The book is teeming with great cinematic elements—a larger-than-life character (definitely a "moose head") and a plot filled with action, sex and tragedy—but two of the three filmizations of the novel missed its essence. Only the 1949 version, featuring Jennifer Jones, is really satisfying. Because no voice-over in the world could provide a decent facsimile of Flaubert's prose descriptions of Emma, any movie version needs to present a *visual equivalent* that shows the character's narcissism and destructiveness through scenes of French provincial life.

You may have to make a similar translation in your script, moving from rendering your characters in the "prose" fashion, toward which you may naturally gravitate, to locating a visual equivalent that will work in your screenplay. Invent as many scenes as you can that place your characters in situations that reveal or act upon their idiosyncrasies or special traits.

What makes a character in a screenplay unique? It's different from what makes a character in fiction unique; screen characters need to be described in a more compressed, visual and overt way. Their idiosyncrasies and other qualities that make them memorable should be demonstrated visually, through their interactions with other characters and within the weave of the story. You might consider including:

- Something physical. How a character *looks*—a trait that separates him or her from other people, and makes him or her feel a certain way because of it (*Elephant Man*, *Georgy Girl*, *Welcome to the Dollhouse*).
- Some intellectual distinction that can be easily expressed onscreen. A particular way of seeing the world, based on certain talents, limitations, etc. (*Good Will Hunting*, *Forrest Gump*, *Rain Man*, *Shine*, *Sling Blade*).
- Some emotional distinction, character flaw or unusual personality (*Terms of Endearment*, *Harold and Maude*, *As Good as It Gets*).
- An obsession (*The Story of Adèle H*, *Les Misèrables*, *Angels and Insects*).
- Intense extremes of love or hate or passion (*The Graduate*, *Damage*).

IMPERATIVE

I explained this point earlier in the chapter, in the context of a character's individual need, but don't forget that there's also the "need" of the movie, too, the imperative that drives the entire contraption, and in which your character is one small but crucial piece of machinery. Make sure that the imperative of the character is in alignment with the imperative of the movie as a whole. Your character is an emissary who sends out the "message" of the screenplay about love, death, sex, family or the fact that there's a giant asteroid hurtling to earth.

Developing a screen character is something that you'll probably be able to do well, because you already know the foundations of character development. (Dialogue, of course, is an essential element in creating character authenticity and expressing the ideas of both the character and the screen-writer. More about dialogue in the next chapter.)

Right now, as you work on your script, make sure that everything you feel or know about your characters actually makes it onto the page in some compressed and clear and specific form. Don't assume that, just because the character has been living inside your head and you've been privately exploring all his or her crevices and peculiarities and com-plexities, these will automatically be transmitted on the page of your screenplay in some subliminal, subtle fashion. When it comes to developing a character, unless the particulars are conveyed literally, they may not come across at all.

You can't rely on an actor to pull all the emotional weight onscreen; a considerable amount of the bulk needs to be on the page to begin with, if only to interest an actor in playing the role. Shirley MacLaine knew she was right for the part of Aurora Greenway in *Terms of Endearment*, because James L. Brooks had written a character that could immediately be identified as larger-than-life, and that clearly appealed to this larger-than-life actress.

You may worry that your entire sense of subtlety has to be thrown away when developing a character in a screenplay. I understand these fears, and I've had them myself, but to some extent I think they're not valid. The kind of nuance that exists on the page need not be thrown away but only translated for the screen, put into the context of drama and action. By all means, strive to make your characters interesting people, memorable and fallible and real, but always make sure the audience sees who they are.

Chapter Seven

Walking and Talking: Dialogue, Action and Putting It Together

One of the things that will be remembered most from your screenplay will be the way the characters speak: what they say, and to whom and why. Here are a couple of crackling lines from movies: "I met a lot of hard-boiled eggs in my life. But you, you're twenty minutes" (Jan Sterling in *Ace in the Hole*). ". . . alligators have the right idea. They eat their young" (Eve Arden in *Mildred Pierce*).

Witty sparring between characters, à la Tracy and Hepburn, gives a crackle to their relationship but is not an end in itself. Individual lines may stand out and be eternally quoted, but what really matters is not exactly what's said but the significance of what's being said in relation to the story. So once again, the skill you may already possess in creating authentic dialogue is helpful, but what's most important is the way in which the dialogue participates in keeping up the momentum.

For most writers, myself included, dialogue is the icing on the cake. It's the part that's fun, the part that you may already know how to do well, because throughout your life parents, teachers and editors have told you that you have an "ear." This metaphorical ear is an extremely helpful thing right now; a screenplay can be a masterwork of architecture, complete with a plot line that commands attention—but if you don't have an ear for dialogue, forget about it.

DIALOGUE

In the most interesting movies, usually more than one thing is going on in a scene; there are often two levels on which the movie is operating, and sometimes two levels on which the dialogue operates: text and subtext. This provides a richness and depth that the audience won't necessarily be conscious of while watching the movie, but if there *isn't* enough going on, then the audience will know it, and will be bored. Each scene should provide something essential—preferably more than one thing. (There will, however, always be necessary scenes that, no matter what you do to them, simply won't shine. Action feels forced and dialogue uninspired. I wouldn't worry about them right now. If they do serve a plot purpose, a momentum purpose, then leave them in for the time being; you can figure out what to do with them later on.) Dialogue is a good vehicle for furthering the momentum of the story, while also showing us who the characters are in relation to each other, and exactly where the friction lies.

Putting three characters into a scene instead of two often makes it more interesting, simply because, mathematically, there are more possibilities. In a three-person scene, for example, character #1 may love character #2, who may feel exactly the same way, but character #3 may love character #1 and secretly despise character #2. Of course, in a love scene you may well want to keep only two central characters, but the action might be aided by the addition of a peripheral character, who serves as a catalyst to ignite the relationship between the others.

Peripheral characters are often crucial in screenplays for exactly that reason; in a way, they can be substitutes for the descriptive and reflective passages that exist in novels but that, for obvious reasons, can't exist in screenplays. Peripheral characters can provide the asides, the explanations and even the moral barometer of the script. The peripheral characters are sort of like members of a very offhand Greek chorus; they can let you know what's really going on, freeing the central characters from having to expound in too literal or self-conscious a fashion.

The topic of dialogue brings up an important question: How do the main characters in a movie talk? Do they sound like you and me? Is their speech riddled with "ums" and "likes"? Or are they more organized when they speak, collecting their thoughts into beautiful, composed salads because they don't have much time in which to capture our attention? In the best of all possible screenplays, dialogue is a combination of both. Your characters should give the suggestion of authenticity without languishing in the mundaneness of genuine-speak, and they need to tell us what's going on in the movie. If what they're saying doesn't further the story, then maybe it shouldn't be said at all, but instead shown visually.

I noted at the beginning of this book that writers' scripts tended to be talky, and I think this common flaw is understandable. We're so used to solving problems and getting out of tight spots through the medium of language that we can't quite believe it will fail us in a movie. But it will. "Talky" screenplays are difficult to love, unless the abundant dialogue is ratcheted up by drama, which is the case in some

Merchant-Ivory films, and in Harold Pinter's scripts for *Betrayal* and *The Servant*, and Penelope Gilliatt's very literate script for *Sunday, Bloody Sunday*.

Rent a couple of your favorite films expressly to listen to the way people in them talk. If blocking out the picture on the screen will help you concentrate on the words, do it. Just as there are visual and emotional "cues" to a character, so are there verbal cues. If a character is a chronic liar, and this is established early on through a memorable moment, then when he speaks later in an important scene, we'll listen to those words with an ear toward discerning whether or not they're truthful. The stakes will be raised because of what we already know, and the words will have a different meaning than they would if we were hearing them cold.

Context is paramount when you're dealing with dialogue. If you go to a restaurant and overhear fragments of drifting conversation from the next table, you might feel irritated at what you hear, thinking one of the people is arrogant or insensitive, or just basically a jerk. But of course you're hearing the conversation out of context, and you don't have any way of knowing how the words fit into the whole relationship between these people. If someone is angry and yelling and waving his breadstick, he may seem like a jerk, but maybe the other person treated him badly, and this is an appropriate response. Maybe the person being yelled *at* is the jerk—or perhaps he's far worse than a jerk. Sometimes the meaning of a scene changes when we're given context; it's occasionally a good idea for a writer to "parachute" down into the middle of a scene, leading the audience to think things are a certain way, only to find out, a little later, that the situation is not at all what it initially seemed.

When two people talk in a restaurant, their conversation isn't fully comprehensible to outside ears because of the absence of real context, but if you pay careful attention, you can learn some important details, such as:

- who these people are in relation to each other
- how well they know each other
- their essential feelings for each other
- what (or whom) they have in common

I always tell my writing students to spend a lot of time listening to the way people talk to one another, being particularly alert to the *shorthand* of relationships, because a version of this shorthand will be used in their work. I once sent an entire class of freshman writing students at Skidmore College to position themselves in various strategic locations on campus in order to eavesdrop on conversations between people and write them down verbatim. My students returned to class the following week and read these conversations aloud as though they were little playlets. (Personally, what I gleaned from this exercise was the pathos of college life; there were so many bits of dialogue about suicidal roommates, insensitive boyfriends, inflexible professors and horrible parents.) After each student read a conversation aloud, the other students tried to guess the relationship between the speakers. One of the main things the class began to see was that people who know each other well speak to each other in an entirely different way from people who have just met.

In a screenplay, an estranged mother and son in a movie wouldn't (or shouldn't) say to each other things like:

STEVE

Hello, Mom.

HELEN

Hello, son.

STEVE

I haven't seen you in . . . how long has it been?

HELEN

Five years.

But they *might* say:

STEVE

Hi.

HELEN

Hi.

STEVE

(Beat) How's Dad doing?

HELEN

He's okay. I'll tell him you asked.

STEVE

Your hair is different.

HELEN

Oh, it's been this way for years.

When writing dialogue, think about the shorthand people use in their conversations. Don't overexplain, but let your characters reveal who they are in relation to one another through their interaction, rather than through the awkward inclusion of fact. Dialogue can reveal both the status of relationships as well as bits of the story. It's okay to let the audience be suspended in confusion briefly; the movement from confusion toward clarity is a perfectly appropriate direction for a scene to take. As a movie progresses, shorthand can be used more freely, because the audience will know more and more, and therefore will have become "insiders" in the contained universe of the film.

How long can you let a character speak? This isn't the floor of Congress; "speeches" are not looked upon kindly in the middle of a screenplay (unless there's a good reason), because they often call attention to themselves and make the enterprise appear false. In life, people don't suddenly stop what they're doing and give an impromptu, uninterrupted speech; other people invariably chime in to contradict or make a joke, or else the telephone rings, or someone gets up and goes to the bathroom. But we're not striving to imitate life here, only to capture and exaggerate it. A longish monologue (half a page, which = 30 seconds) might work fine in your script if it's actually earned, rather than simply foisted upon the audience. And you'll know whether it's earned, because:

- It will come at an emotional moment, at which important dramatic material has been revealed.

- We already know who the character is, and we have very strong feelings about him or her.
- There has been some irresistibly watchable material immediately preceding the monologue, which still resonates.
- The monologue speaks to the larger imperative of the movie.

Here's a sequence from the end of *Surrender, Dorothy*, in which Maddy's mother, Mrs. Bennett—after having been a totally uninvolved mother and disapproving of Maddy's impending marriage to Peter—has a change of heart and unexpectedly returns for her daughter's wedding. I needed to show that these two women were connected in that ambivalent way of many mothers and daughters. I let both characters speak in entire paragraphs, because they were really beseeching each other and trying to convey difficult emotions. If this encounter were taking place in real life, it might sound very different. But I wanted to create a "movie" scene—a slightly heightened interaction that reveals things not just about the way these women see each other but also about the choices they've made and, in Maddy's case, a choice she's about to make.

```
INT. UPSTAIRS HALLWAY — DAY

Mrs. Bennett walks to Peter and Maddy's room
and KNOCKS on the door.


                    MRS. BENNETT
          Maddy?
```

                    MADDY (O.S.)
          Natalie?

She opens the door and sees her mother
there.

                    MADDY (cont'd)
          Oh. It's you.

                    MRS. BENNETT
          May I come in?

INT. MADDY AND PETER'S BEDROOM — DAY

Mother and daughter face each other in the
small room, the bridal dress spread out re-
gally on the bed between them.

                    MRS. BENNETT
          What's going on, Maddy? Where's
          Peter?

                    MADDY
          What do you care, Mother?

                    MRS. BENNETT
1.   I don't dislike Peter. It was
          your father who was upset. It's
          just that . . . we've never had a
          Hebrew fellow in the family be-
          fore, and what was he supposed to
          tell his friends at the club? You
          know your father.

2.   She sinks into a chair.

                    MRS. BENNETT (cont'd)
          Oh, Maddy, I didn't want it to
          come to this. You're my *daughter.*

                         127

I try so hard, but it doesn't
come naturally to me, you know?
It never has, really.

3. She sinks into a sitting position on
the floor. This is the first time this
woman has ever sat on the floor.

MRS. BENNETT

4.
When you were a baby, and they
gave you to me to hold for the
first time, I thought I would drop
you, I thought you would break. I
was terrified. (Beat) I'm also
very sorry about Sara. I heard
about the accident and I just
felt awful. She was a lovely
girl. I always liked her. I remember when we took you up to
Yale, and there she was. I looked
at her and knew that, even though
you were so different, you girls
would become friends. (Beat) I
wanted to call you after she was
killed, but your father felt—

MADDY
My father doesn't control you,
Mother. You're your own person,
aren't you?

MRS. BENNETT
I like to think so. But it's
hard.

There's a pause. Maddy observes her mother
dispassionately, realistically, not unkindly.

                    MADDY
                   (softly)
5. A mother should be there for her
    daughter, okay? Without having to
    be asked. She should just show up
    and do things. She should tell
    her daughter that she thinks
    she's doing fine. She should ad-
    mire things about her daughter.
    She should also boss her daughter
    around a little too, and drive
    her crazy sometimes, and every
    once in a while she should even
    do something totally inappro-
    priate.

                  MRS. BENNETT
    What are you talking about?

Maddy smiles to herself, thinking about
everything she's just said to her mother.

                    MADDY
    Would you excuse me, please?

          INT. STAIRWAY — DAY

Maddy CLATTERS down the stairs.

          EXT. BACKYARD — DAY

Peter is standing with Adam behind the stone
statues.

                    PETER
        I can't let these people stand
        here, waiting for it to start.
        I've just got to tell them.

He takes a big drink from a champagne glass
and then, resolutely, he walks over to the
deck.

                EXT. DECK — DAY

Peter TAPS on his glass with a knife.

                    PETER
        Excuse me, everybody!

The MUSIC dies down.

                PETER (cont'd)
                  (nervously)
        I know a lot of you have come
        from really far away to be here
        today.

                    MIRIAM
                (calling out)
        Wilmington, Delaware! And I'm sup-
        posed to play the lute!

                    PETER
        Look, I have to tell you some-
        thing.

                    GUEST
                (calling out, joking)
        The wedding's off!

```
There's a ripple of LAUGHTER. It stops when
it's clear that Peter isn't laughing, too.


                    PETER
                  (softly)
      Well, yes.


There's a shocked MURMUR among the guests.
Suddenly Maddy comes rushing up to Peter,
her face flushed.


                    MADDY
      Go get dressed.


                    PETER
      What?
```

In this section, we learn something about who Mrs. Bennett is as soon as she starts to speak. When she refers to Peter as a "Hebrew fellow," (#1) we understand that we're dealing with someone narrow and bigoted, but perhaps in an archaic, not entirely conscious way. Next, she takes a seat (#2) and a moment later she sinks down onto the floor. (#3) These small movements are important, because the scene could begin to feel claustrophobic and static if *someone* didn't do something physical. The movements also create a kind of surrender on Mrs. Bennett's part, a noticeable backing-down that gives her daughter the advantage.

In her ensuing short monologue (#4) she becomes more of a vulnerable figure than she was a moment earlier. And Maddy, conversely, gathers more power, coming to a realization about her own mother, and about mothers in general, which furthers the imperative of the script by addressing a few of the script's central, implied questions: What should a mother's role be in her grown child's life? How much should mothers and daughters tell each other? How close is too close? (#5)

Interesting questions ought to be raised by the dialogue in your screenplay, and something always needs to be conveyed by the dialogue—either by what's being included, or by what's left out. For instance, you might have a scene in a movie in which all the characters are playing a fast and loose game of poker, and what looks like merely an evening's entertainment is actually a way that the characters cope with some trauma, which is gradually revealed through the dialogue of the poker game.

Never let your characters speak in a generic way. There is no such thing as a "generic" person, except in a bad movie. A specific and unusual predicament is not enough to propel a movie forward—the characters and their words need to carry a significant amount of the burden. All your characters need to be specific, with speech patterns that will both reflect this specificity and clarify it for the audience.

Here are a few dialogue exercises that you might try as you work on your script:

1. Write a monologue in which your character reveals his or her biggest secret (as identified in the Character Questionnaire in the last chapter) to someone else. Feel free to let the other character speak in response.

2. Write a page of dialogue between two of your characters in which a couple of important facts are revealed, without anyone actually coming right out and stating them.

3. Write a "toast" that your character might give at a wedding or some other kind of celebration. (Getting comfortable with this kind of "formal" speechmaking is helpful when writing dialogue, since all speeches in a movie are in effect being given to an assembled crowd, even though the object, during the movie, is to forget that fact.)

4. Come up with a "catchphrase" that each of your central characters would say, even if you don't use it in the actual screenplay.

5. Watch a pivotal scene involving dialogue from one of your favorite movies. Write down some of the dialogue word for word. What makes the scene so memorable? How does the dialogue contribute to that effect?

As with all the other elements in your screenplay, the more you practice, the more your dialogue will improve. If you are a playwright, your dialogue is no doubt already superb, and you probably should have skipped this section entirely. There's not a clear-cut distinction between stage and screen dialogue—except perhaps that screen dialogue is shorter—but there is a definite distinction between "written" and "spoken" dialogue.

Finally, the best advice of all is to speak your dialogue aloud, to act it out in the privacy of your own room, when no one is around to mock you. It's difficult to make phony dialogue said out loud sound natural, and chances are that you will do a fair amount of editing after you really get a chance to hear the words you've put into your characters' mouths.

ACTION

Forward motion, propulsion, momentum—these are all words that pertain to the action of a movie. But action doesn't only refer to the large movements; it's also the small bits of "ordinary" business that accompany dialogue. Nicole Holofcener's 1996 movie *Walking and Talking* is about two best friends whose relationship changes when one of them announces she's getting married. The whole movie is very low-key, and about as low-concept as it gets, and most of the "events" center on the characters literally walking around and talking about things. The "action" isn't seismic, but it is persistent, because we always feel some shift taking place in the friendship.

The characters, played by Anne Heche and Catherine Keener, are believable and their dialogue authentic. In an idiosyncratic but representative moment, one friend leaves a message on the other's answering machine, and in the middle she babbles to her friend that she's standing there smelling a sponge, which smells oddly like a hot dog, and she can't seem to stop smelling it. Through the combination of fresh dialogue and action, the women help carry the poignant, even profound theme of the movie to its conclusion.

I love the title *Walking and Talking* and think you might do well to keep it in mind as you try to combine action with dialogue. Everyone in your movie should always metaphorically be walking and/or talking; nothing should ever come to a complete halt, or the movie will in effect lie down and die on the spot. Keeping a screenplay in motion for 120 pages is like being a contestant in the *They Shoot Horses, Don't They?* dance marathon; you have to keep your feet shuffling for much longer than seems humanly possibly. This task is made much easier by the combination of a good treatment, a thorough understanding of your characters, a definite sense of the imperative of the movie and, most of all, *practice.*

Your first screenplay will probably be less than perfect. It will be imperfect in ways that you won't be able to discern for a long time, perhaps not until you've written your fifth or sixth screenplay. But your writing will definitely get better the more of it you amass, which is a statement that I wouldn't routinely make to my fiction students. I don't operate under the belief that anyone can write a good short story if they keep trying. But I do think that most people can write a decent screenplay eventually, if they really study the three-act structure and generate ideas that will work well within that structure.

Some screenplays are brilliant conceits, with terrific and original story lines but without any real, memorable characters to speak of. Some have strong characters but not a lot of story. Others, like *Pulp Fiction*, are inventive and exciting *and* populated by interesting characters. *Pulp Fiction* registered with audiences as very compelling, and it's not really hard to understand why. Some critics complained about the grotesquely casual treatment of violence, but others saw this as representative of the culture at large. Either way, it gave audiences something to talk about over dinner after the movie was over, and it did so not because of any one particular element—not even John Travolta's brilliant, creepy comeback from mediocre-movie purgatory (conversations with a wisecracking unborn baby in *Look Who's Talking* and its desperate spawn *Look Who's Talking Too* and *Look Who's Talking Now*, not to mention movies you've never heard of such as *Chains of Gold* and *Shout*)—but because of its characters, story and the fact that Quentin Tarantino has something that every writer wants: voice.

VOICE

It's entirely possible to have a good "ear" for dialogue, and a good "eye" for the visually compelling moment, but no "voice." Voice is the thing that makes a script feel like no other. Voice is the thing that makes a script the talk of the town and turns a "weekend read" into a Monday-morning bidding war. Here's a short list of movies that have a strong voice behind them:

> *Good Will Hunting*
> *Tender Mercies*
> *Strangers on a Train*
> *Annie Hall*

Compare the above with the following movies, which have no discernible voice, and which could have easily been written by committee:

> *Three Men and a Little Lady*
> *Conspiracy Theory*
> *Air Force One*
> *Addicted to Love*

This latter group includes the hollow movies you sometimes see on airplanes, or the ones you rent at the video store because everything good has already been taken. Unlike structure or plot points or momentum, voice isn't something you can learn to master. Your voice, if it's there, will have been in place (even if it's a bit muted) since you began to write years ago. This isn't to say that you can't write a decent script without a voice, but it certainly helps if you have one.

Luckily, you're already a writer, and chances are that you've already got a voice, and you know exactly what I'm talking about. While you can't learn to develop a voice if it's not there, you can be reminded of something that many writers seem to forget: Never think that you should "dumb down" or commercialize your ideas, merely because you're writing a screenplay. When you write a script, don't throw away the qualities that make you most interesting as a writer. In fact, apply the relevant things about your writing that make it good when you venture into scriptwriting. Be as idiosyncratic as you really are; don't hold back or set out to make a story more slick or mainstream. That kind of thinking rarely works or pays off. If you're the kind of writer who isn't particularly slick or mainstream, don't try to mute your voice, or it will sound like everyone else's, and will never be heard. The only thing you probably *should* try to make like everyone else's is the structure of your screenplay. Studio executives are a lot more forgiving of unusual material if it comes in a package they recognize: three acts, 120 pages. The rest is up to you. Let yourself do what you do best.

Chapter Eight

Ways of Working: Habits, Rewrites and Collaborations

Another question that writers are often asked—after "Where do you get your ideas?"—is "How do you work?" A few years ago at dinner parties, everyone was always eager to know if a writer used a word processor, but now no one bothers with that question because it's assumed that we're all hooked up to computers, and that our fingers fly across the keyboards like those of the most seasoned hacker. This is certainly true of screenwriters, who need a computer and appropriate screenwriting software to do the job. But the question of "How do you work?" extends beyond whether or not you use Macintosh or Windows, or Final Draft or Scriptor. The question also concerns your work habits: how much time you put into the enterprise each day, how much time it takes overall to finish a script, and how you know when you're working on something for too long, and ought to give it a rest.

Essayist John McPhee has mentioned having to tie his bathrobe belt to the back of his chair in order to force himself to keep writing, and I think all writers understand this resistance to the work. There's rarely an *ease* to writing, an endless fountain of available material, and this is certainly true for screenwriters. The necessary brevity of scenes and attention to structure create a situation in which you're forced to start and stop, then start and stop again. (This choppiness helps explain why so many people are drawn to the index-card approach; it lets the writer think of the screenplay as a short stack of scenes, quite the opposite of the endless "scroll" of paper that Jack Kerouac put into his typewriter to write *On the Road*.)

How do you stay focused for a long time on such a start-and-stop project as a screenplay? How do you maintain the discipline to work within the structure, and the patience to go back over scenes as many times as they require? I have a certain method of working which won't suit everyone, but here it is: I try to keep banker's hours, working from the morning to the afternoon. I'm not a teller in the bank—I consider myself a vice president—which means I have some power and can decide to knock off early one day if I want to, or take a little snooze. I am disciplined with myself, but not overly strict. I feel extremely lucky to have such a wonderful job, and I know that it has to be tended to, or else I will grow lazy and my imagination fallow.

When writing a script, you should continue to follow the same sort of schedule you already follow as a writer, but be sure that you find a chunk of time and a place to work that's totally private, so you can feel free to pace the room, plaster the walls with index cards if you need to, and say dialogue out loud. The freedom to talk to yourself is essential. Sometimes it helps to act out a scene with a close friend, listening for whether or not the cadences feel natural. You might also try "pitching" the idea for the movie to your friend, à la *The Player*, explaining the premise and a few of the compelling details as though to a studio executive. If you can't be coherent and comprehensive in five minutes' time, then it's possi-

ble that your script needs some tinkering to make it more coherent and linear. At some point in the process you may want
to show everything you've written so far to your friend. A
fresh eye can really help, especially when you've been working on something nonstop for a long time.

A TIMETABLE

How long is too long to spend on your screenplay? Here's a
suggested timetable for the various phases of script development, as well as some tips about working during each phase.
While all writers work at their own pace, this schedule
should let you know whether or not your expectations are re-
alistic:

- **Generating an Idea: An indefinite amount of time.**
  Old ideas are often recirculated much later, after they've
  been reconsidered and reconfigured in your mind. But if
  you decide you want to turn an idea into a script, don't start
  the treatment until your idea is solid. Watching movies and
  reading scripts really helps during this idea-gathering
  phase, as well as thinking of what genre you'd be happiest
  working in.
- **Treatment: One to two weeks.** Don't spend too much
  more time than this. Perhaps an extra week might come in
  handy, but I'm afraid if you work on it too long, you won't
  want to move on to the actual script. Use your writing skills
  here to their best advantage, being sure to lay down all the
  major points.
- **Script: Six to eight weeks.** (Does calling it "two months"
  give you the psychological advantage by making it sound

longer?) If your treatment is as strong as it ought to be, then you should be able to complete a draft of the script within this period of time. Of course, life often intrudes: kids get strep, bills need to be paid, and sometimes you get stuck on a particular scene and it throws the entire process off. If you're stuck on one scene for more than two hours, move on to the next scene, and then return to the difficult one later.

- **Reading Period: One to two weeks.** This is an important and extremely enjoyable phase of the screenwriting process, because there isn't so much pressure on you to create or remedy as there is to *evaluate* and take some notes. Looking at a draft of your own work objectively can be eye-opening, and more so than ever when it's a form that's new to you. You'll be able to see your tics, your pet phrases, the shocking number of times you repeat the same adjectives. You'll be able to see your flaws more clearly than when you were writing the script. None of these flaws and weaknesses should be too alarming, because you'll soon have a chance to generate a second draft.

- **"Taking a Breather" Phase: One to two weeks.** I'm serious about this. It's not that I fear you've become so overwhelmed by work that your fragile constitution needs a *Magic Mountain*–like rest cure; it's only that you've been living with this script for a concentrated period of time, and there's no way you can really see it clearly right now. You've probably practically *memorized* all the words, and you've become wedded to your scenes and story and characters. You need to remove yourself from the premises for a while, doing something totally different from writing and reading scripts. By the time you return to your screenplay, you'll be able to look at it more clearly and dispassionately. Ideally, when you return, the script will seem as though it had been written by someone else, and that you've only been hired to do a rewrite. Wait until there's a slightly unfamiliar quality to the writing, until it isn't so fresh and beloved (or loathed) by you. Wait until you can slash and burn your way through it again, which is what many rewriting processes entail.

- **Rewriting Phase: One to four weeks.** A rewrite can be as uncomplicated as a brushing-up of dialogue to a total slash-and-burn overhaul, as mentioned above, which in Hollywood parlance is known as a "page one rewrite." It all depends on what your particular screenplay requires. (More on rewriting a little later.)

WORK HABITS

The attitude you take when writing a screenplay ought to be disciplined but flexible. Sometimes "work" involves the pleasurable task of renting *It Happened One Night* and watching it in the middle of the day, or else buying a copy of the collected screenplays of Woody Allen and studying them as though preparing for a big exam. Sometimes you'll find you can't solve a particular problem in your script, and you don't know what to do about it. Some writers pack up the tent when this happens, stopping work for the day and hoping that the problem will be miraculously solved while they sleep.

I tend to think a problem ought to be addressed at the point that you experience it most acutely. Don't spend hours and hours on a scene that's going nowhere, but do try to fix a broken scene or section of a script by running down this checklist:

- reminding yourself of the imperative of the script
- thinking about the "name" you've given the act, and asking yourself whether your characters and their environment fit within this description
- looking to the treatment for answers

If you still can't clarify what's wrong and fix the difficult section of the script, then I suggest you create a temporary poultice—a quick, less-than-perfect version of the material that allows you to move on, with the understanding that you'll come back later and fix it.

I like to examine the actual pages I've written, so I create hard copy very often. There's something commanding about having the real page in front of you, which even a page-sized computer screen can't quite provide. Print as often as you need to, in order to get a sense of how the script reads. Your goal is to generate a script that is well written, well paced, well organized and compelling. While sometimes you can detect glimmers of these qualities in a first draft, it's far more likely that you'll have to wait until after the rewrite to feel truly pleased with what you've done.

THE REWRITE

I consider rewriting one of the most essential phases of writing, regardless of the form. As a novelist, I am infinitely helped by revision. If, God forbid, I were to die after completing a first draft of a novel, and my publisher decided to print it as is, I would roll over in shame in my grave. Revision gives you a chance to redeem yourself, to recognize your errors and change them before anyone else sees them. You will probably find plenty of missteps in your screenplay: scenes that go on far too long, not to mention pointlessly; characters who speak like Stepford wives when you were aiming for naturalness; an intended "emotional" moment that falls flat.

What should you do when the scales have been lifted from your eyes and you can finally see what's wrong with your script? If I were simply to reply "Why, fix it!" that would be like a therapist telling a distraught patient to stop feeling sorry for herself and buck up. Fixing a script is an exercise that more often than not requires objectivity, patience, heartlessness, stamina, and an influx of fresh ideas. As you read back over what you've written, don't be afraid to mark the entire thing up, to reorder scenes, to give one of your characters a different job or a new motivation, if the old one suddenly seems stale or unhelpful.

The kind of thinking that governs rewriting is essentially the same as the kind that governs *writing*. The only difference is that now it's not only theoretical; you actually have an entire text to work from. You'll find scenes that feel exactly right, and that help further the imperative of the script; *don't touch them.* Some writers tend to pick and pick at everything they've done, and without realizing it they can unravel the fabric that holds the whole thing together.

What you *should* be tinkering with, however, are the scenes and sequences that aren't vibrant. If something in your script isn't evocative—if it doesn't provide its readers with a feeling, a *sensation,* a way of thinking about the world that the script has created—then rework it. Sometimes what a scene needs will take less work than you might imagine; occasionally it requires that you remove a chunk of dialogue, or perhaps bring in another character to increase the activity onscreen as well as the mathematical possibilities for emotional dynamics.

If you aren't sure what your script needs, and reading over your treatment yet again isn't helping, then give the script to a friend. Let your friend be the judge. You may be at the point at which you really don't know why something isn't working; perhaps you have a generic sense that "it sucks," but you can't be more specific than that. Sometimes an outside person can read a script and instantly see the problem, and might even suggest what he or she would prefer to see in a particular scene.

If you're a very private writer who doesn't enjoy having others read your work or offer advice, you ought to rid yourself of these tendencies now. They were fine when you were in your Proustian phase and sitting in your cork-lined study peering at your work through a monocle, but the nature of screenplays is (eventually) collaborative, so you'd might as well get used to other people's opinions and impressions now.

If your friend reads your screenplay and announces either that he or she likes it or doesn't like it, try to get a few more specific responses. You could ask, for instance:

- What would you say the screenplay is "about"?
- Did it seem to you to have a good story?
- Did you like the characters? Why or why not?
- Describe the "mood" of the screenplay.
- Were you ever bored? At which parts?
- If you could change one thing about the script, what would it be?

It will be interesting to compare your friend's responses to your own original conceptions of the script. It's not essential that they match in every way; an outside read can sometimes give you new insight into an unconscious strand of the script. Readers do, of course, have their own agendas when they approach someone else's material. Sometimes they misinterpret wildly. My tenth-grade English teacher told my class that the title *The Old Man and the Sea* was made up of six words, each one three letters long, and that since $6 \times 3 = 18$, and 18 in Hebrew is associated with the word "chai," which means "life," Hemingway's novel was an affirmation of life! Listen closely to what your friend says about your script, but don't lose sight of what you know to be true about your own work. (And whatever you do, don't let my old English teacher get her hands on your script.)

Some scripts cannot be fixed no matter what you do to them, and this may be because of a fatal, congenital flaw that somehow couldn't be detected until now. Every writer has this experience at some point or other, and I've taken the attitude that it's simply par for the course.

A failed script should not be regarded as having been a waste of time. Instead, it is extremely useful. I'm not one of those people who generally regard tragedies and loss as "learning experiences." I don't really see the need to interpret something that is, by most objective measures, sad or traumatic as also being "good," just because you made new friends when you went for your chemo after you had breast cancer, or because you learned to be a fighter after you were brutally mugged, et cetera. But a failed script isn't tragic, and it isn't even a real loss. It *is,* actually, a learning experience. You ought to realize that you needed to write that script in order to be able to write one that would be better—one in which you would never make the same mistakes again.

Never throw away a failed script. The bones of it can be picked over years later, and perhaps even made into screenplay soup—by which I mean that even the worst script by a good writer has bits of charm in it. You can pillage from the scripts you put aside, and this includes not only the failed ones but also the good ones that, for some reason, you aren't able to sell—which is an unfortunate but fairly common experience that simply comes with the territory.

COLLABORATING

For me this word still has bad associations; I can't help but immediately think we're talking about World War II and the Nazis. But even the kind of collaborating we really *are* talking about—the kind where two writers work together— makes me somewhat uneasy, because it seems to go against the grain of the fact I learned about writing when I was young: that it's something you do by yourself.

To writers who are used to forms that don't lend themselves so naturally to collaboration, the idea of sharing the burden of work with another person seems either like something that would take a lot of getting used to—rather like three-way sex, or a bicycle built for two—or else like a great reward after so many years of writing in isolation. It may be a difficult transition to make, but collaborating with another writer whom you like and trust can be a terrific experience. It all depends on the chemistry of the personalities involved, and the specifics of the project.

Some kinds of ideas seem to do well being written by more than one person, and these tend to be "big" ideas, the sort that might just be too unwieldy for you to manage on your own. Historical screenplays or other kinds of scripts that require a great deal of research, interviews or actual field-work might be helped along by a second writer. You can divide the workload and exchange ideas. Engaging in a dialogue with another person is often extremely useful when trying to come up with and develop an idea in the first place.

I've recently begun a screenwriting collaboration with novelist Peter Smith, who is smart and funny and likes the same kinds of movies I like. We sometimes meet for an "ideas" lunch, to toss around our thoughts about the sorts of projects we think we'd enjoy working on, and figure out how to turn them into solid, three-act ideas that can be translated into screenplay form. Generally, we start from the outside and work our way in, by which I mean that we discuss what kind of writing mood we're in: the mood for romantic comedy or serious drama. (Those are pretty much the limits of our repertoire right now; maybe the Hong Kong action-adventure scripts will come later.)

Peter and I spend a lot of time talking about movies we've seen lately, and why, to our way of thinking, they either "work" or "don't work." I tape-recorded the beginning of our most recent lunch, in the hopes of being able to provide a window into one type of collaboration. We talked generally about screenwriting, and about what would make a good film, and somehow the free associations of the more general conversation led to, at the end, a specific idea:

M: So, what genre this time? How about . . . romantic comedy?

P: (laughing) Fine. We don't do anything else.

M: I'm glad I collaborate with a man, because we can draw on so-called male experiences, and maybe the movie actually has a chance of getting made. Once in a while a "women's" movie gets made, but it's really an exception. So let's think of a world that can include men, and can also feel like an actual, separate "world." Something we have experience in.

P: And it should take place someplace where we've lived, or that we know a lot about. A world we understand. Maybe an interesting job would be a place to start.

M: Have you ever had a job?

P: (laughing) Yes, in fact I have had a job. In publishing. And my first job was at a Wendy's. I wore the shirt, I wore the regulation pants, I wore a button that said hot and juicy, with my name underneath it. I lasted two months.

M: So maybe a movie that combines publishing and fast food.

P: It's a shame to me that so many of the great stories you hear—for example, my mother marrying her high school boyfriend at age sixty-nine—would never sell. Because the characters are too old.

M: It could be on the Lifetime Channel.

P: Yeah, with Louise Fletcher. Because the characters aren't twenty-five- to thirty-five-year-old males.

M: How can we write a movie that can get made? That's the question we're always circling. A movie that we actually like. I refuse to banish older characters—characters who don't fit the demographic. But I want to write something that can be produced.

P: We were talking recently about how honoring "normal" people in this country seems to be a very big issue in movies, whether it's *Forrest Gump* or *Mr. Holland's Opus*. Our culture is so overcome with notions of accomplishment and fame and wealth. But from the very beginning of *It's a Wonderful Life*, a movie that really struck a chord (although when it first came out it was considered a dud) we see that there's something there about honoring the unexceptional, the regular. How one has an effect on one's own life, on one's own friends.

M: And even if you were to write a movie about a prince, you would want to see that he was like us in some way. You'd like to see that the Dalai Lama was once a pretty regular little boy, who liked cartoons. Sometimes I think to myself: if I were writing a novel, I would never stoop to this level. But it's not exactly "stooping." We're trying to write a movie that a studio will buy, and will spend millions of dollars on. It's not a game, or a charity project. And I'm afraid that, for the most part, there are rules. And you have to learn them, unless you're one of the very few people who are exempt.

P: And the rules are, what? First find a character you can love?

M: Sort of. But probably not within a "character-driven" movie. You want a plot-driven movie.

P: Because it's all about story.

M: Right. And not a language-driven movie, either. Because there's really no such thing. The ideal here, at least for writers like you and me, is a plot-driven movie with a character people respond to.

P: Now how did they get around that in *As Good as It Gets*, with such an unlikable character?

M: Well, I think they got around that because he was Jack Nicholson. I don't think they could have gotten around it if there had been an unknown playing that part. The thing is, everybody was excited that Jack Nicholson was playing such a shit. That was interesting to people. Also, the invective that he spewed spoke to the American sensibility, in a way. And the awfulness of his character was counterbalanced by the niceness of the other two characters. Nicholson is awful, but we see his—oh, I hate this word—vulnerability. He's got obsessive-compulsive disorder, he's pathetic, he's not just a monster. He's humanized, even with all his awfulness. It's always a question of balance: Nice and not so nice. Light and dark. You're always balancing elements in a screenplay.

P: I don't think we should ever forget about casting. It's an important factor.

M: Yes. We need something with great roles that will make actors want to be in it. Something specific.

P: And a specific setting. Preferably not New York.

M: Right. But it *could* be New York . . .

P: You run the risk of people feeling hostile to the movie, because they're often hostile to New York. It has to be a place that people understand. They need to know what it feels like to live there. You and I have both lived in other places—different cities like Houston, Boston—

M: And you even lived in Australia.

P: Yes, oddly.

M: (laughing) We could do a movie about . . . marmite. People who work in an Australian marmite factory.

P: We've both lived in academic communities, too.

M: Yeah, the *Goodbye, Mr. Chips–Dead Poets Society* universe.

P: I think they're appealing in movies—it's like a little village, the same way that a hospital is. A self-contained world.

M: And just like in a novel, people like to see characters change.

P: As we know in our own lives, of course, people really just don't change very much, although a thousand therapists would drop to the floor to think that.

M: And a thousand producers, with their "arcs."

P: In both novels and screenplays, we like to see the flight toward change. For some reason, I fear that people look at novelists who want to write screenplays and think they're being cynical. Because suddenly what they're doing is "for" somebody. An audience. A studio.

M: But that doesn't make it easy. It's not cheating.

P: No. The hardest lesson I've learned is that I have to give the same amount of time and attention to a script that I would to a novel. I look at a script and I see 120 pages; I see all this air and white space on the page, and the inclination is to say: Give me a long weekend; I can do that. But it just doesn't work that way. *Star Wars*—not my favorite movie—took two and a half years to write. Most of these movies go through something like thirty-two, thirty-five drafts.

M: There is something to be said for already being comfortable around writing. People who want to write a script and who haven't written anything before can be very cowed by the actual writing. They don't know what to do.

P: Not that writers always know what to do, either. But the territory of written ideas is at least familiar to them.

M: And it gets more familiar the more you do it, the more ideas you come up with, and try, and then toss out.

P: Sometimes something sticks. I'm thinking, here, of what we were saying about that self-contained world. What about the world of actors?

M: They're pretty interesting. Everyone wants to know about them.

P: Young actors trying to make it in New York.

M: Right. And the nice thing is that they're not all "New York types," whatever that is. They're from all over, and they've come to New York to try to have a career. They're imports. People can relate to them—they're from the America they recognize, and they have ambitions.

P: And it's castable. Good parts for actors.

M: Ethan Hawke as . . . a struggling Ethan Hawke.

P: Okay. Let's start mapping out the three acts.

Say you decide you want to collaborate with someone on a screenplay. How do you decide whom to work with? I generally think writers who are friends work better rather than stranger-writer duos who have hooked up purely for a project. Friends know each other's cadences and rhythms and strengths; friends know each other's sensibilities. You should choose a friend with whom you get along well, and with whom you don't have a lot of "issues." (I don't think I need to explain that further, do I? If you've got a lot of issues with a friend, both of you will know it. An "issues" friend is the one you complain about in therapy, and with whom you still get into tense, awkward arguments that sometimes end up in tears.) Peter is a friend with whom I have no "issues"; we're close but respectful of each other, and we have separate spouses, children and lives. We enjoy being together, and we laugh ourselves sick. Most important, I value him as a writer; he's primarily a novelist too, and his fiction is rich and complex and always interesting.

An ideal collaborator is someone whom you generally like and respect as a writer. Both of you might be new to screenwriting, but you will both have some real writing experience behind you, so that there's a parity to the relationship. It's perfectly all right for one of you to be the de facto "leader," the one who's better versed at writing in general or screen-writing in particular, but you must see your roles in this enterprise as equally important, and be willing to listen to each other's ideas and complaints with respect and consideration.

It's also not a bad idea if the two of you are "complementary" writers in some way—if one of you has particular strengths in an area where the other one is lacking. In our case, I am very happy to let Peter write all the dialogue between two male characters; I feel that he can do a better, more natural job at it, so it stands to reason that this should be his territory. As for me, I handle the female stuff (I'm embarrassed by how typically gender-based these decisions are, but I have to say our work seems to come out the best when we divide it this way) and can give conversations between women characters a naturalness that Peter might not have been able to. (Jane Austen famously said that she never wrote a scene in which only two men talk to each other, because she didn't know what men say without women present.) Figure out what you and your partner do best, and where your individual interests lie.

Suppose you want to work with a friend and together you come up with a terrific idea, but you're not sure how exactly to collaborate. The writing phase of collaboration can be executed in different ways; one of them will feel right to both of you, and that's the one you'll choose. Peter and I have a certain way of working that satisfies both of us and draws on our strengths as writers. We create a treatment together, fifty-fifty, meeting over lunch and hammering it out roughly, then discussing it further on the telephone and e-mailing each other our ideas. When we've jointly created a treatment that we feel happy with, we move on to the first draft.

Some collaborators divide up all the scenes in an act, as in

"You take the opening sequence in the motel, and I'll take the death scene in the supermarket," or "I'll take all the love scenes because I'm a sucker for that kind of thing, and you take all the action scenes because you're definitely more into those kinds of movies and understand how they work." Then the writers go to their separate homes and work on the scenes. Because they know (from the blueprint of the treatment) where the scenes will fall within the three-act structure, and what role they will play in the movie, they know exactly what must be accomplished in those pages. When the writers are satisfied with what they've written they swap pages, making necessary editing suggestions and corrections, and then they move on to the next set of scenes, working back and forth in this manner until an entire act or script is completed.

Because I often fantasize about having extended, undivided time to let my writing unravel—and because I'm not of the start-and-stop, index-card school of screenwriting—the collaboration method I've just described isn't really for me. Peter and I work another way entirely. When we have finished our joint treatment, one of us (usually Peter) goes home and takes a crack at a huge chunk of the script, perhaps the entire first draft. When he's done with that, he shows it to me and I rework it, so that the finished product has a lot of his sensibility in it and a lot of mine. I prefer to have him write the first draft because I think he's better at overarching structure, and I'm better at creating the smaller changes and nuances within a scene. I guess you could say he's the first-draft writer and I'm the person brought in for the rewrite, but both of these tasks are formidable, and the choices we make as writers are largely culled from our initial conversations about the script as well as from the treatment we have prepared together, so the project really does end up being totally collaborative.

You and your writing partner ought to both agree up front (and put it down on paper) that if you sell your script you will split the money fifty-fifty. Even if one of you seems to be doing "more" than the other, screenplays go through a long, long process from the time they are begun to the time they are produced, and both of you will need to feel like equal partners who can call upon each other for help along the way without worrying about who's doing how much based on your respective percentages of the deal. You should behave as a united front—it's more professional that way—and this starts with the financial agreement.

Not all scripts can or should be written collaboratively. Sometimes two voices joining together negate the "voice" of the script entirely. If your screenplay is particularly idiosyncratic and unusual and stems from a vision that belongs to you alone, then don't try to enlist anyone else to help you with the writing; that script is *yours*, and maybe the reason you want to collaborate is because you're frightened that what's "yours" won't be good enough. Risk taking, of course, is an essential component of all forms of writing; the scripts that don't try to do anything new or interesting—the ones that just want to please everyone with their hollow, sitcom sensibilities—are the ones that feel generic and should be avoided.

Would you ever try to write a great *novel* with a friend? It's doubtful. But you might collaborate with someone on a potboiler that you write under a pseudonym. Good screenplays are the equivalent of neither great novels nor cheesy ones; they are a different entity and need to be tackled differently from the start. It's hard to create art with another person, but it's less hard to create craft, and screenwriting is a craft. Another plus to writing with a collaborator is that you have a built-in sounding board, someone who knows every turn and nuance of your script, and who can talk about it with you ad infinitum, which is probably more than your significant other will do. (Collaborating with your significant other is something you might want to avoid, unless your relationship is unshakeable.) A collaborator is a witness to all the different parts of writing a screenplay—the pleasures and the seemingly endless difficulties—and he or she can also take a bit of the sting out of the writing process, and now and again even provide a few necessary laughs over lunch. The agent who handles my screenplays generally isn't in favor of writing duos, because he thinks the "voice" of the script is in danger of getting watered down. He may be right, and if you and a friend do decide to work together, be sure that the writing feels as strong as it would have if only one of you had written it—or better yet, stronger.

Chapter Nine

From Fiction to Film: Adaptations

There are times when the idea you've come up with for a screenplay is not your own. You may stumble upon an old, out-of-print novel from 1953 at a garage sale and immediately know it would make a great movie. The scenes are vivid, the characters unique, and the overall story is mesmerizing. Or maybe the novel or short story that you feel would make a great movie is one you've written yourself. These are different experiences, of course, but there are some pieces of advice that apply universally.

Adaptations are, by nature, extremely difficult, because you have to reconceive material while still being true to it. But in some ways they can be easier than working with original ideas, because much of the hardest work has already been done for you. When I first began work on the screen adaptation of my novel *Surrender, Dorothy*, I was wary. After all, I'd just finished the novel, and now I needed to go all the way back to the beginning and pick apart everything I'd done. Once I made my peace with this idea, I was able to approach the project without the dread I'd been feeling. What kept me going was the idea (erroneous, it would turn out) that while in some ways I would have to reimagine the novel to make it work as a screenplay, for the most part I would be able to remain fairly faithful to the original. After all, most of the adaptations of books or stories that I'd seen and liked had been pretty true to their sources: John Huston's version of Joyce's *The Dead*, or *To Kill a Mockingbird* or *Giant*. When I sat down to write my script, I thought I was in fairly good shape; I had something much better than a treatment from which to pilfer—I had an entire novel.

But the first draft of the screenplay of *Surrender, Dorothy* didn't work. Flat, vague and without a lot of action, the script needed to be scrapped and reimagined. This, of course, was a dispiriting exercise, and I couldn't shake the idea that I had somehow failed. (By the time this book is published, the project may be in production, still alive but not yet produced, or perhaps completely dead. Its fate may have everything to do with my abilities to truly create something new and structurally sound out of previously existing material, or it may have nothing to do with my abilities whatsoever.) Jane Rosenthal, my producer at Tribeca Films, kindly suggested that perhaps the first draft had been a way of getting the novel "out of my system," and now that I had done so, I could proceed with the project more effectively. The novel itself couldn't really be broken down into three discrete acts (which should have been my first inkling that it needed a great deal of restructuring in script form), so I had to recast the whole thing—a daunting notion even when the material isn't your own.

My producer thought that I should basically forget most of the book as I wrote the screenplay. This idea might be offensive to many writers, but it wasn't to me. I'd made peace with what was in store for me; I'd adopted a cheerfully resigned "caveat scriptor" attitude, and could take comments and criticism. The first act—in which the character Sara is killed and then her mother, Natalie, moves into the beach house of her grieving friends—could stay, we agreed. The action in the early chapters of the novel made for a solid first act (although I had to lose most of the character backgrounds and digressions that I'm so fond of as a fiction writer. But after this "act" ended, I had nowhere to go. The novel becomes much more contemplative and elegiac after the dramatic opening events; these qualities, if left unconnected to actual *movement,* would probably sink my screenplay. I needed to find a way to set the "clock" ticking all over again and give my characters—and, for that matter, the entire movie—an imperative. At first, this was an impossible chore, one which I dreaded. Day after day I would return to the adaptation, keeping the manuscript of my novel open on the desk beside me as I worked, constantly referring to my own words as I went along, desperately needing John McPhee's bathrobe belt to tie me to my chair.

Finally I realized that I ought to put the novel away while I wrote the screenplay. This was difficult for me to do; it felt as though I was on a trapeze without a safety net. Most people doing adaptations work closely with the original text, but I had the sense that the text was holding me back, keeping me doggedly faithful to something that was not in my best interest. I could hold on to the overarching idea of the book— the characters, the story line in its roughest sense and the tone—but the rest was up for grabs. To work this way, without constantly referring to the novel, would be tough, but maybe doable. After all, I knew my own book well enough— both the characters and their predicament. Without the imposing, inviolable-as-the-Torah presence of the novel in front of me, I somehow found myself able to write the script more freely and become less protective of the original material. *Surrender, Dorothy* would still be inviolable as a novel, but clearly the screenplay would have to be done differently, or not at all.

So my producer and I came up with the idea of a wedding. Ceremonies can provide terrific moments in screenplays because they include some very cinematic elements: visual excitement, a heightened emotional state and sense of drama, and a chance for characters to speak their thoughts eloquently in a way they aren't often allowed elsewhere. Ceremonies in movies can be funny, moving, bristling with characters, music, dancing, flirting and small asides, and they can create a terrific sequence that people will remember.

We decided that building toward a wedding on a specific date would set the clock ticking again. And so my characters Maddy and Peter—who in the novel are married and have a baby—would in the movie be engaged and about to get married. I planned an end-of-movie wedding for them, lavishing thought and time on it, choreographing the small moments and the big, sweeping ones much the same way I would do if I were writing fiction. Soon we had an entire new plot worked out, and it felt much more satisfying as a potential movie than what I had laid out in my novel. Some writers would find the process of this transformation too painful to undergo; I completely understand this hesitation or even distaste, and, in fact, for just this reason I think it's usually best for someone else to adapt your work.

But if you're going to be the one doing the adapting— whether it's your own work or another author's—one of the most difficult tasks you'll face is freeing yourself from the bonds of the original material and reconceiving it in a way that will lend itself better to a screenplay. Some original material seems to be virtually "pret-a-porter," and you'll have a predictably smooth time writing a script from it. Such material tends to be clearly, simply drawn and with a strong plot. But most novels, stories, articles and plays require a great deal of remodeling before they can be translated into a decent movie.

If you have material you've written in another form that you think would make a great movie, chances are you already own the rights to the material. (This may not be true if it's a profile of a famous person or if it "borrows" actual events, for which you may need to obtain permission. If you have a literary agent, check with him or her before even beginning such an adaptation.) Many "classics" are available for adaptation without having to be optioned for a sum of money, because they were published so long ago that they've fallen into the public domain. Again, you'll need to check with your agent, or make inquiries on you own, contacting the publisher of the most recent edition of the work.

How do you know whether a piece of writing would make a good screenplay? At the very least, it should have:

- a strong story
- unusual characters
- a visually interesting setting

It needn't have all three acts in place to begin with, but if it doesn't, then you'll have to provide them. Sometimes this involves creating new characters, altering the setting or the time frame, or even changing the story around. Be careful if you're thinking of adapating a work that has entered the public consciousness; remember the failed Demi Moore version of *The Scarlet Letter*, which had an absurdly chipper ending?

And if you're adapting a play, be sure not to let the screenplay have the stagy, theatrical quality of many film adaptations of plays. (*The Boys in the Band*, *Butterflies Are Free*). The best way to translate a play into a movie, to release it from the confines of the stage and open it up fully, is to give it plenty of scenes in diverse settings.

Like most writers, I have a devout reverence for books, and I cringe when I see something great tortured and mucked up for the screen. But I don't mean to encourage a stodgy allegiance to the material; such reverence has produced dull movie missteps such as *Ethan Frome*, and *Where Angels Fear to Tread*. I'm not so much of a purist that I don't believe adapatations should be made. Why not introduce a whole new audience to a film version of some wonderful piece of writing? Often, moviegoers will actually read the book after seeing the movie. There's even a place for fast-and-loose interpretations of the classics; the Claire Danes–Leonardo DiCaprio version of *Romeo and Juliet* had a vibrancy and a vision, even though it seemed to be most clearly intended for teenagers.

When you're writing an adaptation, you need to do so with a kind of "translated exactitude." The term *adaptation* implies change, interpretation, perhaps a shift in emphasis. (Art borrows from art; if you want to be reminded of this age-old concern, read Harold Bloom's *The Anxiety of Influence*.) You have to understand the heart of the material you're working with, so much so that you are free either to create a "replica" in screenplay form or to go far afield (perhaps even alarmingly so, to devotees of the work), but still be true to the essential aesthetic and meaning of the original text. The Basil Rathbone Sherlock Holmes movies from the 1940s are gems that kept the wit of Sir Arthur Conan Doyle while imbuing the stories with a wonderful, elaborate sense of Holmes's character, thanks to Rathbone's clever interpretive skill. The movies in this series have a winking, knowing quality—more playful, even, than the original material, yet very much true to the source.

If you're thinking of adapting a piece of writing, you'll need to find ways to take what is interior about it and make it exterior. Long passages of silent reflection in a novel can be translated into dialogue (not word for word, though; people don't speak in such fluent passages). And scenes merely alluded to in the novel in a sentence or two can be expanded and given new weight. The direction an adaptation must take is *outward*—moving toward what can be seen with the naked eye and easily felt. A movie is *not* an intellectual exercise. Although some of the best ones are intellectually rigorous, they are that way almost parenthetically. Without a successful structure and vivid scenes, setting and characters, the intellect will be buried under confusion and dullness.

Sometimes, a novel, play or story that you absolutely love does not make a good screenplay, because what you love about it irrevocably resides in the interior realm. With *Surrender, Dorothy*, I was lucky enough to get to keep most of my characters (after altering a few important details about them). But after my character Sara's death at the beginning of the novel, I had to change almost all of the action in order to create a screenplay that was not about language but about a story and its momentum.

Chapter Ten

Sending It Out and Moving On

A protective bubble surrounds the writer until it's time to show the script to somebody who will pass professional judgment on it. It's one thing for you to think you've done a good job (or for your mother to think so) and quite another for someone to think you've done such a good job that he or she wants to pay for your services. But it does happen; scripts by unknown writers are sold all the time, sometimes for great sums of money.

The first thing to do when you've finished a script is to make sure it looks good—that the format is right, and that the pages aren't peppered with careless errors or typos. Neatness does count; a sloppy script raises the possibility that the author is a sloppy writer, and the script may be read less seriously than it would have been if it had been meticulously typed and formatted. You want your work to look good, without putting in any little extras—forget about fancy typefaces or graphics.

After your script has been carefully proofread and gone over with an eye toward zero-hour changes, you must register it with the Writers' Guild. This is essential, as it protects you from someone else claiming that the script (or the idea for it) is his or hers. You can either bring or send your finished script into the offices of:

> Writers' Guild of America, West
> 7000 West Third Street
> Los Angeles, CA 90048
> or:
> Writers' Guild of America, East
> 555 West 57th Street
> New York, NY 10019

But call first for instructions, and also to find out the registration fee, which varies, depending on the length of the project. You can also register your script on line: The Writers' Guild Web site (http://www.wga.org) is very informative about registration and other legal concerns screenwriters face; you will need to become a member of the guild when you sell your first script. (You can't join until you've sold something to a guild signatory.)

After you register the script and are ready to send it out, have it bound with fasteners and a plain, simple cover that features the title, then beneath the title the words "a screenplay by" and your name. In the lower right-hand corner, type your address, telephone number and the date. That's all; don't put anything about "copyright" on the cover; this just makes you look like you don't know what you're doing. I give my fiction students similar advice when they're sending out a manuscript; none of that "First North American Serial Rights" business on the title page, or how many words the novel or short story is. Just type the thing, put on a title page, and send it off.

But to whom should you send your screenplay? If you already have a literary agent, then this is a conversation the two of you should be having. Most literary agencies work with an in-house film agent or a West Coast branch of the agency that handles film, or else they farm these duties out to a theatrical agency that works with them—sometimes a major presence such as CAA. Ask your agent what he or she does about screenplays. If there's someone who would be right for you to work with, make sure your script gets shown to this person.

If you don't have a literary agent who can point you in the right direction, then you'll need to find a film agent on your own. While this is a difficult task, it's not impossible. It's not as though agents are hiding from talent, or turning down real talent when they see it. Unlike other fields such as acting— where there might be hundreds of actors who are perfectly competent to play a single role—the field of screenwriting is not crowded with brilliant material. Most directors feel that much of the material they are sent—and this means scripts written by seasoned writers represented by big agents—is mediocre. So when something special comes in, everyone gets excited.

If you happen to have a friend in the film business, you might ask him or her for the name of a good agent. A personal connection helps; it will probably get your script read more quickly. (It could also get your treatment read, if you haven't yet written the script.) If you don't have any connections, then contact the Writers' Guild for their list of agents. On this list, you'll find names of particular agents who are willing to read scripts that come in "over the transom," that is, unsolicited. Read carefully the information about the agencies and specific agents, and choose two or three to contact, either by a phone call or by a simple query letter that includes a one-line description of the kind of writing work you've done in the past, and then perhaps a very short phrase describing the genre of your script, as opposed to a long detailing of its plot. Here's an example of the kind of letter you should be writing:

> Dear _____,
>
> I am a fiction writer who has published short stories in *The New Yorker* and *Harper's*, and I have written a screenplay that I would like to send for your consideration. *Bay Parkway* is a drama set in Brooklyn during World War II, about a young girl's relationship with her neighbors who have lost a son in the war. If you would be interested in reading it, please let me know, and I will send it along. Thank you very much.
>
> Sincerely,

A query letter establishes a few things: who you are and what you've already done professionally; what your new project is; whether you're crazy or sane. I'm not kidding about this last point; a query letter can be annoying or vaguely inappropriate or even over-the-top, and such a letter lets the agent know right away that he or she should stay away from this writer. Your letter should be short and courteous and neatly typed. If the agent turns you down, it may be because he or she just doesn't have room on his or her roster for another client. But there are plenty of young, hungry agents out there who respect talent and are eager to cut deals. You don't need to go to a "name" agent; it may be much better to have an energetic one. It's perfectly okay to send out more than one query simultaneously. Once an agent has agreed to read your screenplay, send it off with an SASE (a stamped, self-addressed envelope; you know the drill) if you would like it returned. If you don't need it returned, indicate as much in your brief cover letter.

You may have to contact many agents before you find one who's willing to read your script, and even when you've found such an agent, he or she may very well not choose to represent you. Agents generally only want to represent a writer they feel passionate about, or one they recognize as a surefire moneymaker. They don't want to go to bat for a mediocre writer or a half-baked script. Finding an agent can be a slow process, and a read might take up to six or eight weeks. (If eight weeks pass, you're within your rights to give the agency a call and ask about the status of your script, as it may have gotten lost in the shuffle of material that passes through the office.)

If you do find an agent who likes your script enough to want to represent you, it will be understood, either through verbal or written agreement, that he or she will act on your behalf and will take a percentage of any money you earn as a screenwriter. An agent is a necessity if you're writing screenplays, since he or she can arrange contacts for you with producers and studio executives, as well as handle the complex legal language of your contracts. So don't even think of acting as your own agent; that's sort of like Long Island Rail Road killer Colin Ferguson and serial killer Ted Bundy serving as their own lawyers in court. And look how much success they had.

If your screenplay is repeatedly rejected (ten rejections

equal "repeatedly," in my book) then it's time to consider whether you ought to put it aside and start something new. (Actually, in the best of all possible worlds you would have already started something new by the time you send a script out for consideration.) Never grow too attached to one screenplay; screenwriters complete dozens of them in their lifetimes. Your next script can use elements of your first one. Each time you write, you can "borrow" the good stuff from your scripts that nobody wanted, until finally all the elements seem to be working and somebody says yes. Some writers quickly become discouraged; they think they're not cut out for writing screenplays if the first or second one isn't immediately sold. But I think this is fallacious reasoning; unlike fiction writing or poetry, which can't truly be "taught" without the presence of an innate and profound talent, screenwriting *can* be taught to talented writers. It's just a matter of being patient and becoming well versed in the form, combined with understanding the vagaries of the marketplace.

If a film agent does decide to represent you, there are several paths he or she might take with your script. It isn't an analagous situation to the publishing industry, where when you hand in a novel to an agent, he or she will submit it to several publishing houses. A film agent may well decide to send your script to a producer first, so that this experienced person who has a good relationship with one or more studios might want to be "attached" to the script. Or your agent may want to send the script to a particular actor first. If a major star shows interest in your script, a studio will jump at the chance to make this film. (Coming soon: *Bay Parkway*, starring Tom Cruise!) Or your agent may want to attach a specific director to the project, which could once again put you in a strong position, especially if the director is someone with real clout. An agent may, alternatively, submit your script directly to the studios, sending it to every studio for a one-shot "weekend read," which means that an executive from a studio takes it home over the weekend and either makes an offer or "passes" on Monday. Or the agent may decide to be a bit more measured and send it out to only one or two studios, carefully gauging the response before proceeding further.

There are various possibilities for a "spec" script, and when you have an active screenplay that's being shown around, it's a very exciting and nerve-wracking time. I don't really want to discuss potential money here, because the range of payment is wide, depending on a variety of factors, such as:

- whether a major studio or an independent company is putting up the money
- whether more than one studio is bidding and the price gets driven up
- whether the script is "optioned" (rendered exclusive to the studio for a specified period of time) or bought outright (the studio then owns it).

You'll stay in constant touch with your agent during the period when your screenplay is being shown around, but if he or she is someone you like and trust, step back and let the agent take charge.

MOVING FORWARD

Writers usually don't start feeling like screenwriters until they've written at least two scripts, possibly three. Like any other new skill, writing screenplays takes on an ease and grace the more you do it. A successful screenwriter I know has at least a dozen unproduced screenplays in her file cabinet. Probably anything she were to write now would be optioned or bought, but back when she was working on these scripts, she hadn't made a name for herself and just kept doggedly moving forward. She was always in the middle of something, always dreaming up a new idea. There was never a sense of failure on her part, or of wondering whether she was a "natural." Few people are naturals, exactly. Some are quicker studies than others, and if you are one of the lucky ones who immediately and intuitively understands the relationship between form and content in the screenplay, you may have a success early on.

But screenwriters always need to reinvent themselves. Each screenplay is different from the last one. Your next script will be better, richer, more complex, more relaxed. If you can find a way to work screenwriting into the rest of your life—devoting enough time to it so that you can give a script the attention it needs (and they all need a lot of attention)—then you will become good at it. Some writers say that they find writing screenplays a kind of recreation, so different is it from the other work that they have to do. If you've spent a lot of time doing various kinds of writing, experimenting and following your own instincts even as they led you toward four thousand-word prose-poems or one-woman monologues for the stage, it may in fact be a relief to have to bow to the structure that a screenplay demands, and still get to keep your own voice and style and the other elements that make your writing unique.

Your script is your own. No one can take it from you (as long as you've registered it with the WGA). But you do need to possess a kind of resilience, an indefatigable quality and a desire to continue figuring out what the form requires. It's like an elaborate riddle of the Sphinx, in which the answer can be found only by using one key: structure. The beauty of the script, the sensibility, the humor, the originality: all that comes from you alone. My screenwriter friend was right to stay flexible and to keep moving forward.

This is what every screenwriter needs to do. Love your writing, but not *too* much. Keep screenplays separate from the rest of your writing, clearly delineating time for scripts from time for all other projects. And keep the ideas separate, too; try not to let notions for screenplays bleed over into the rest of your work, and vice versa.

I recently started working on a new piece of fiction, and a friend of mine who had read the opening pages commented that it read like a treatment for a movie. I was horrified and embarrassed. But as I looked back over what I'd done, I realized that my friend was right. The pages provided a beat-by-beat overview of the beginning of the novel, describing everything that happened rather than letting the reader feel as though he or she was immersed in the experience. I had never had this problem before I began writing screenplays, and I'm sure it happened because briefly I "forgot" whether I was writing fiction or film.

After this experience, I was reminded that I needed to be more vigilant. I also realized that I needed to go back and reread the writers who have inspired me and made me want to be a fiction writer: Virginia Woolf, Philip Roth, Grace Paley, Willa Cather, John Cheever, Elizabeth Bowen, James Joyce, Anton Chekhov. None of these writers' work reads as though it was meant for the screen. As Richard Price suggests, fiction is about language. "Story" is more important to some of these writers than to others. When I oriented myself in the world of the fiction I loved, I was able to shake free of the movie demons that sometimes haunt me and my prose.

Lately, when reading novels I've become very sensitive to fiction that has a "screenplay" quality about it; the prose is too simple and declarative, the action is too swift and the interior life of the characters has not been developed satisfactorily. I'm never surprised when I learn that the writer has worked in film. On the other hand, some writers strengthen their work when they become fluent in writing screenplays— in particular, writers who in the past have had trouble grasping the idea of story or momentum.

It's hard to predict whether or not your fiction, journalism or plays will change because you've begun writing scripts; it all depends on the kind of writer you were to begin with, and whether you're disciplined enough to segregate the different sides of your writing life, or flexible enough to apply some of the good story lessons of screenplays to your other work. When word processors became ubiquitous some years ago, most of the writers I know began to realize that these machines were affecting their work, making it possible for them to write longer sentences, longer paragraphs, longer *books*. And because editing became so much easier, too, these writers started to do much more self-editing than they were used to. An initial impulse to write something one way was abandoned in favor of another impulse, which was then abandoned in favor of yet another impulse, so that the initial (and perhaps best) impulse was long forgotten under a mountain of revision. (When I took my SATs in high school, my mother warned me that the first answer I came up with was probably right, and not to erase it.) But despite the potential pitfalls, almost every writer I know uses a word processor; as they say in medicine, "the benefits outweigh the risks."

The same is true when writers try their hand at screenplays. Screenwriting can be creatively and financially rewarding, and if you're inclined to try it don't hesitate. While you will need to segregate your film side from the side of you that produces the other kind of writing you do, don't ever try to separate out the different parts of your writing sensibility. You're yourself, for better or worse; your sensibility has been fully formed and the clay has cooled, long before the time you decided to try to write a screenplay. Don't contort yourself into something you're not when writing a script—don't try to write like a Hollywood screenwriter, taking on a layer of slickness that you think the form requires. It doesn't. Of course it's perfectly okay to think shrewdly and to be aware of what kinds of movies actually get made. Screenwriters owe it to themselves to see plenty of movies, both the good ones and the bad ones, and definitely the commercially successful ones, if only to figure out the logic of what's going on in the minds of working screenwriters and the studio executives who hire them. Many movies of our hypercommercial era have become inextricable from the bloated culture of advertising and excess, a fact that is painfully difficult to ignore, yet the cynical imagination can never create a movie to be proud of. Be aware of what movies often are like today, but don't try to contort yourself to fit into a niche in the industry.

Hollywood will always need good writers; it's as simple as that. Be smart and aware, but never be false. I don't even advise this for moral reasons; I mostly mean that a false script will not fool anyone. If you keep your own sensibility—the purest essence of who you are as a writer and what moves and amuses and obsesses you—then your script will be original. Your truest self should always be right there on the page, whether you're writing a novel about a wealthy, elegant and elliptical man named Jay Gatsby, or a blockbuster screenplay about a race of violent androids taking over Las Vegas. If the structure is in place, the writing is memorable, the characters are vividly human and the sensibility is very much your own, then you're all set.

Epilogue:
Q & A

Writers who are just beginning to delve into screenplays seem to have similar questions about the field of screenwriting, so I thought I would include the ones that get asked the most often:

Q: I came up with a great idea and I wrote a treatment and then just started writing the script. But it's going nowhere. How do I know when to keep staying with it, or when to quit?

A: No one can tell you what your breaking point is. A writer should stay with a project as long as he or she can tolerate it. You surely already know that much of writing—any kind of writing—isn't pleasurable, that a great deal of time is spent in frustration and in unraveling difficult problems. But when you're writing a screenplay and you have some sort of treatment to refer to as you work, then you ought to be able to tell if the problem lies in the original conception, or in some failure of imagination in making the treatment come to life. In short: Is it the idea, or the execution? If you figure out that it's the idea, then you'll need to let it go gracefully, or else start from scratch in reconceiving it. But if the idea still seems solid and you feel that your writing just isn't up to par, it may be time to reacquaint yourself with scripts—how they read, and why they work or don't work. Get the scripts of some films you admire and which fall roughly into the same genre as yours. It's fair to say that many well-written screenplays have a similar "feel" to them. (I would never say this about novels or other forms of writing.) It's hard to define this quality; it has something to do with a smooth readability, a sleekness, a polished surface and a snap to the dialogue. Perhaps these screenplays have a distinctive "voice." Take a look at your own script and compare it to these others; what's missing? A good script is seductive. It should leave the reader with a particular feeling. It should resonate.

If you're having a lot of trouble with a script, you might want to join a screenwriters' workshop in your area (inquire at the Writers' Guild, or at a local film school). Unfortunately, there are times when a screenplay just doesn't work no matter what you do to it, and you must step aside. It may be a case of a poor match between writer and material. Or it may just be that you're not quite ready to tackle this particular script. Never throw anything away; you may choose to go back to a difficult screenplay at some later point.

Q: My first act is really good, but my second act is a mess. What can I do?

A: This is a common problem. While some writers only hit their stride in act two, others run into trouble when the first act ends. These writers will be tooling along, really enjoying the process, building characters and situations and dropping in plot points, and then suddenly somewhere between page 20 to 30, the whole enterprise starts to fall flat.

By nature, second acts are less contained and simple than

first acts. They have to cover a lot more material; they have to tell the bulk of the story. Second-act problems are akin to the problems writers have in other forms; basically, beginning a piece of writing can be a pleasure, but once you get into the thick of it, the thrill has faded and the characters seem like people you've lived with for far too long. Remind yourself that there are only 60 or so pages in the second act, and that you have a great deal of ground to cover. There's a lot to be done; this isn't an idle, leisurely act at all. Remind yourself of the imperative of the script, and remember that the second act is literally and figuratively the heart of the whole movie. Making a second act seem lively and exciting is a big job; you cannot "coast," or the act will become sluggish.

Sluggishness on the part of the writer is often the culprit when the second act goes badly. If you've just spent a considerable amount of time completing a strong first act, you may simply need a break. Go do something else entirely; I give you permission to knock off for a whole week, and try that tough second act again.

Q: Do I have to have actors in mind for all my leads?

A: Yes, kind of. Don't let it dominate your thinking, because that would be a cynical way to go about the enterprise, but it is a good idea to be able to think like a casting agent, at least some of the time. This piece of work you're doing isn't meant to stand on its own; it's simply a blueprint for a movie. The characters should suggest real people who can actually play them. If you don't want to narrow yourself down too much, you might think of a character as a Leonardo Di-Caprio *type,* which essentially means boyishly (okay, girlishly) good-looking and lean and cool and of a certain age. Sometimes having actors in mind actually helps you know your characters better, in that it puts into your head a voice that might speak your lines. Along with that voice come gestures and subtle bits of business, too.

Q: At the risk of sounding crass, what kind of screenplays are actually getting sold these days in Hollywood?

A: If there's one particular type of script that seems to sell more easily than others, it's the big, slick, cleanly written action picture—a high-concept screenplay that's long on event and short on other things. An action picture that's explosively exciting and actually has real characters in it and better-than-average dialogue gets executives interested.

There are two types of screenplays: those that are viewed by studios as gigantic moneymakers, and those that aren't. It's tough to get people excited about a script that doesn't fall into the first category, but it can be done. One way is to write a vehicle for a star. Peter Weir's *The Truman Show* is a high-concept nonaction movie directed by a prestigious director that was turned into an event by the presence of Jim Carrey.

What kind of screenplays attract stars? Generally, screenplays that feel "the same, but different." Scripts that offer the stars big, unusual, bravura roles. Occasionally an actor likes to play against type, perhaps to portray someone decidedly unheroic, such as Ralph Fiennes's SS commandant in *Schindler's List*. Tom Cruise's ambitious, flawed sports agent in *Jerry Maguire* was a surprise turn for the actor, and it worked. Cameron Crowe's script was intelligent and charming, and Cruise understood that this would work to his advantage.

Castability is a major factor in getting a script made. If there aren't parts in your script for males between the ages of twenty-five and forty-five, you may have to forget about going the mainstream route. A screenplay "feels" like a movie when there are great parts for actors—especially men. Good parts for women are important, too, but usually they need to be reinforced by the parts for men. It's a depressing but unavoidable fact.

Supposedly, every studio longs to develop romantic comedies, but generally these need to have some kind of strong concept behind them (*My Best Friend's Wedding*) or else they will fade away.

High concept, of course, is the direction to go if you want a better chance of your script getting made. But well-written and exciting are vital traits, too. Once in a while a script comes along that isn't particularly high concept but that has a certain winning, Oscar-potential quality, and these often are bought for large sums of money.

As always, write about the things you care about and know about. But do it in a cinematic way.

Q: Is there any advice to give to writers who are starting their first screenplays?

A: Do it because you love movies and want to see if you can make some money writing them. It would be a shame if you thought screenwriting was the way out of all your financial problems, because it's not. Writing and rewriting a single script can take a long time, and you need to be patient and able to pay attention to craft. Also, cynicism is a bad trait. While I advocate knowing what's out there, and understanding what a saleable movie is, I would never suggest that you write something you didn't care about. It's not that you'll hate yourself in the morning, as you wake up in your new L.A. mansion—but that you probably won't be waking up in a mansion, because your script will lack authenticity and vigor.

If you're a good fiction writer or playwright or journalist, think of the best reviews your work has gotten; what did the reviews say about your work? And what would the equivalent praise be, if you were writing a screenplay? Your scripts will be different from your other work, but the voice behind them should be yours.

RECOMMENDED VIEWING

This is a short list of movies that I think about when I think about screenwriting. While none is obscure and you may in fact have seen all of them, you might want to take another look now that you're writing scripts yourself. Some of them have been included just because the writing is so good; others have been chosen for more specific reasons. It is by no means a comprehensive list, but instead a starting place. Make a short list for yourself of other movies that include notable writing, and see if you can identify what made their screenplays so memorable.

All About Eve (1950): Intelligent, sophisticated script about backbiting theater world.

Dead Man Walking (1995): Two-person character study is heartbreaking and raises complex moral questions.

Fargo (1996): Atmospheric and propelled by chilling Coen brothers' wit.

Holiday (1938): Though based on a play, this satisfying Katharine Hepburn vehicle has a wonderful, funny and moving script that makes it feel like a movie, not a play.

I Know Where I'm Going! (1945): A love story without a lot of plot, but it works as a simple, touching tale.

McCabe and Mrs. Miller (1971): Gorgeous Robert Altman film combines intelligent writing with bleak atmosphere.

RECOMMENDED VIEWING

Mildred Pierce (1945): Intense mother-daughter noir film. A character study of a woman (Joan Crawford) that also has a suspenseful story.

My Dinner With André (1981): Breaks all the rules mentioned in this book and fascinating in its own way.

Nashville (1975): Notable for its deft handling of several different related stories.

Raging Bull (1980): Brilliant film of deeply unappealing character (Robert DeNiro), via Scorsese.

Rear Window (1954): The device of James Stewart's broken leg sets this murder mystery in motion.

Shadow of a Doubt (1943): My favorite movie ever. Hitchcock's look at the darkness at the heart of Americana has a script by Thornton Wilder and is bristling with characters and beautiful cinematic moments.

The Shawshank Redemption (1994): Stephen King's shaggy-dog-story prison movie feels like a novel you don't want to put down.

Since You Went Away (1944): Conventional but affecting World War II premise that tells a simple, straightforward story with likeable characters.

Some Like It Hot (1959): One of the funniest films ever made, of course, with wonderful dialogue.

Sunday, Bloody Sunday (1971): Smart film of sexual triangle has the textured feel of a novel.

Sunset Boulevard (1950): Interesting use of flashback in this dark, wicked Hollywood story.

RECOMMENDED READING

These books are all, in different ways, "cinematic," by which I mean they seem to lend themselves to the screen—in some cases very obviously, in others less obviously. Several of these books have, in fact, been turned into movies (I've put an asterisk [°] next to them). Think about how the books differ from their adaptations. If you were to adapt one of these books for the screen, what changes would you make? (In particular, the Salinger titles are of interest because in real life they will never be adapted; Salinger won't allow it. But you can try to adapt them in your imagination.) Again, this is only a short list off the top of my head, and not meant to be inclusive.

Giovanni's Room, by James Baldwin

The Sweet Hereafter, by Russell Banks°

Chilly Scenes of Winter, by Ann Beattie (as *Head over Heels*)°

The House in Paris, by Elizabeth Bowen

Villette, by Charlotte Brontë

Civil Wars, by Rosellen Brown

Mrs. Bridge, by Evan S. Connell (as *Mr. and Mrs. Bridge*)°

Stop-Time, by Frank Conroy

The Waterfall, by Margaret Drabble

RECOMMENDED READING

Heartburn, by Nora Ephron°

As I Lay Dying, by William Faulkner

Postcards from the Edge, by Carrie Fisher°

Final Payments, by Mary Gordon

The World According to Garp, by John Irving°

The Turn of the Screw, by Henry James (as *The Innocents*)°

Then She Found Me, by Elinor Lipman

Foreign Affairs, by Alison Lurie

Memories of a Catholic Girlhood, by Mary McCarthy

Sula, by Toni Morrison

The Catcher in the Rye, by J. D. Salinger

Franny and Zooey, by J. D. Salinger

In Dreams Begin Responsibilities (title story), by Delmore Schwartz

Anywhere but Here, by Mona Simpson

Mrs. Palfrey at the Claremont, by Elizabeth Taylor

The Age of Innocence, by Edith Wharton°

BOOKS ABOUT SCREENWRITING

While much of the advice in them does seem geared to beginning writers, the following books are extremely useful in many ways, especially in their thoughtful discussions of structure. The original Syd Field book, *Screenplay*, in particular, is considered the classic screenwriting manual, and it's helped countless people learn to write scripts.

Four Screenplays, by Syd Field

The Screenwriter's Workbook, by Syd Field

Screenplay, by Syd Field

Story, by Robert McKee

Making a Good Script Great, by Linda Seger

PUBLISHED SCREENPLAYS

Most of the scripts I've read have been in unpublished form, with three holes punched in them and held together by fasteners. But screenplays of produced films are often published, and the following is a very short list of some books that might be useful to look at while you're starting to write.

Hannah and Her Sisters, by Woody Allen

When Harry Met Sally, by Nora Ephron

Four Screenplays, by William Goldman

The Company of Men, by Neil LaBute

Lolita, by Vladimir Nabokov (this is *not* the script that Stanley Kubrick filmed)

The Proust Screenplay, by Harold Pinter (currently out of print)

Three Screenplays, by Richard Price

Moonstruck, *Joe Versus the Volcano* and *Five Corners*, by John Patrick Shanley

SCREENWRITING SOFTWARE

Computer technology tends to advance with such swiftness that pretty soon you'll probably only have to think up an idea for a screenplay while staring at a specially treated photograph of Michael Eisner, and within minutes it will turn into a camera-ready script to be produced by Disney. But until that happens, here is a list of recommended software programs on the market—the ones that format rather than form your ideas for you (the latter is a product that I still find extraneous but that some writers really do find useful, especially during rewriting, claiming that it's like having a writing partner).

Final Draft (This is the software I use; it's simple to understand as well as to install and comes with two separate sets of disks so you and a screenwriting partner can both use it.)

Movie Magic Screenwriter

Script Thing

Scriptware

If you need to talk about your script software needs with a knowledgeable and friendly person, the place to call is the Writer's Computer Store, located in Sausalito, California. Their phone number is 1-800-272-8927, and you can ask them to send you their catalogue, or order items over the phone.

ACKNOWLEDGMENTS

I'm very grateful to the following people, who have all generously helped give me a crash course in screenwriting: Jody Hotchkiss, Geoffrey Sanford, Nora Ephron, Mark Saltzman and Peter Smith. In addition, I'd like to thank the wonderful film editor Arnold Glassman, who knows more about classic movies than anyone I've ever met, and who shared his expansive knowledge with me.

FOR THE BEST IN PAPERBACKS, LOOK FOR THE (penguin logo)

In every corner of the world, on every subject under the sun, Penguin represents quality and variety—the very best in publishing today.

For complete information about books available from Penguin—including Puffins, Penguin Classics, and Arkana—and how to order them, write to us at the appropriate address below. Please note that for copyright reasons the selection of books varies from country to country.

In the United Kingdom: Please write to *Dept. EP, Penguin Books Ltd, Bath Road, Harmondsworth, West Drayton, Middlesex UB7 0DA.*

In the United States: Please write to *Penguin Putnam Inc., P.O. Box 12289 Dept. B, Newark, New Jersey 07101-5289* or call 1-800-788-6262.

In Canada: Please write to *Penguin Books Canada Ltd, 10 Alcorn Avenue, Suite 300, Toronto, Ontario M4V 3B2.*

In Australia: Please write to *Penguin Books Australia Ltd, P.O. Box 257, Ringwood, Victoria 3134.*

In New Zealand: Please write to *Penguin Books (NZ) Ltd, Private Bag 102902, North Shore Mail Centre, Auckland 10.*

In India: Please write to *Penguin Books India Pvt Ltd, 11 Panchsheel Shopping Centre, Panchsheel Park, New Delhi 110 017.*

In the Netherlands: Please write to *Penguin Books Netherlands bv, Postbus 3507, NL-1001 AH Amsterdam.*

In Germany: Please write to *Penguin Books Deutschland GmbH, Metzlerstrasse 26, 60594 Frankfurt am Main.*

In Spain: Please write to *Penguin Books S. A., Bravo Murillo 19, 1° B, 28015 Madrid.*

In Italy: Please write to *Penguin Italia s.r.l., Via Benedetto Croce 2, 20094 Corsico, Milano.*

In France: Please write to *Penguin France, Le Carré Wilson, 62 rue Benjamin Baillaud, 31500 Toulouse.*

In Japan: Please write to *Penguin Books Japan Ltd, Kaneko Building, 2-3-25 Koraku, Bunkyo-Ku, Tokyo 112.*

In South Africa: Please write to *Penguin Books South Africa (Pty) Ltd, Private Bag X14, Parkview, 2122 Johannesburg.*